Singing with Emmanuel

OTHER TITLES BY CHARLES D. DREW

The Ancient Love Song: Finding Christ in the Old Testament

A Journey Worth Taking: Finding Your Purpose in This World

Surprised by Community: Republicans and Democrats in the Same Pew

Singing with Emmanuel

How to Meet Jesus in the Psalms

CHARLES D. DREW

Foreword by Tremper Longman III

WIPF & STOCK · Eugene, Oregon

SINGING WITH EMMANUEL
How to Meet Jesus in the Psalms

Wipf & Stock
An Imprint of Wipf and Stock Publishers
199 W. 8th Ave., Suite 3
Eugene, OR 97401

www.wipfandstock.com

PAPERBACK ISBN: 979-8-3852-6646-3
HARDCOVER ISBN: 979-8-3852-6647-0
EBOOK ISBN: 979-8-3852-6648-7

VERSION NUMBER 02/19/26

All italics in quoted verses are the author's emphasis.

For Avy, Violet, Micah, Hannah, and Amarachi,
my favorite young people.

Perhaps this book will help you share with me something of the joy of Aslan's Great Story, in which every chapter is better than the one before.

Contents

Foreword

The book of Psalms is the hymnbook of the Old Testament. Its one hundred and fifty songs celebrate God (hymns), bring our struggles to him (laments), thank him for hearing us (thanksgivings), and express our trust in him even in the midst of pain (confidence psalms).

The psalms were written for public worship but can also be used for private devotion, as templates for our own prayers. As the historical titles indicate, like the one that identifies Ps 51 as a prayer of David after he sinned by sleeping with the married Bathsheba, they were written out of specific events in the composers' lives but in a way that later worshipers can pray them in similar, though not necessarily identical, situations.

In this, as John Calvin taught us, they are "mirrors of our soul." The psalms as a whole express every emotion that a human being experiences and bring them to God. Israel's hymnbook thus becomes our prayer book. It gives us the prayers that, as we make them our own, arouse our emotions, stimulate our imaginations, inform us, and appeal to our wills.

Charlie Drew knows that the psalms were Israel's and our songbook, but he insightfully reminds us that the psalms also point us to Jesus. In his words, "They all, in one way or another, bring us to Jesus." Notice that Charlie puts the emphasis on "all" the psalms, not just a handful that are frequently quoted in the New Testament. Jesus himself pointedly told his disciples that the entirety of Scripture (the Old Testament) anticipated his coming (see Luke 24:23–27, and note especially 24:44).

The psalms are both songs about Jesus and songs that Jesus sings. Charlie notes how the New Testament authors report that Jesus used the psalms to express his heart. He expresses his profound suffering on the cross by uttering the first verse of Ps 22: "My God, my God, why have you abandoned me?" (Matt 27:46). The Gospel of John (2:17) tells us that, when Jesus cleansed the temple, his disciples saw him as displaying the "zeal" or "passion" that the psalmist expressed in Ps 69:9.

But Charlie rightly tells us that we should imagine Jesus singing even psalms that were not cited in the New Testament. We should thus read them as Israel's songs, our songs, and Jesus' songs. Wonderfully, Charlie not only tells us we should read them as such, but he guides us through a number of psalms to illustrate his important point.

I have known Charlie for about fifty years, going back to our seminary days. He is brilliant, a clear and passionate writer and speaker, and a person who loves Jesus. All this comes through in this well-written and insightful book. I commend it to all readers and particularly to those who teach and preach the Psalms.

Tremper Longman III, PhD
Distinguished Scholar and Professor Emeritus of Biblical Studies
Westmont College

Preface

Listening for Christ's voice in the psalms, what I have sought to do in *Singing with Emmanuel*, is by no means the only approach that people have taken. But it is one with a rich and ancient tradition going back to Origen (AD 185–254), Jerome (AD 347–420), and Augustine (AD 354–430). They all sought to meet Jesus in the psalms, an approach that grew out of their method of Bible reading in general. Hans Boersma describes that method:

> When the Fathers read the Scripture, they entered it by way of concentric circles. They began with the very center, Christ himself. Christ himself was the measuring stick, the canon, for all interpretation of Scripture. He, the Person of Christ, was the rule of faith or the canon of truth, on which the faith was based and by which all biblical reflection should be measured.[1]

This ancient approach continues into the present. Contemporary Old Testament scholar Bruce Waltke, as summarized by Graeme Goldsworthy, asserts that "the Psalms . . . stand as the prayers of Jesus Christ who, as the corporate head of the church, represents all believers in their own prayers."[2]

I trust that Augustine will inspire you as he has me: "It is Christ's voice which ought . . . to be perfectly known and perfectly familiar to us in all the Psalms—now chanting joyously, now sorrowing, now rejoicing in hope, now sighing in its present state, even as if it were our own."[3]

1. Boersma, *Hermeneutics*, 12.
2. Goldsworthy, *Preaching*, 202.
3. Brown, *Augustine*, 257–58.

Acknowledgments

I owe great thanks to many for their encouragements, endorsements, and constructive criticisms. Among them are Old Testament scholars Doug Green (who called my attention to the ancient "Vox Christi" tradition my book evokes), Peter Lanfer, and Tremper Longman III; church and educational leaders Frank Guerra, John Howe, Tim Keller, Niel Lebhar, and Peter Moore; campus ministers Jim Black, Tom Cannon, Larry Christensen, Kevin Neimann, and Ava Ligh; authors Amy Julia Becker, Mardi Keyes, Kathy Keller, and David Powlison; parishioners Grace Kim and David Yum; and my children, Allen and Sarah. Thanks to Laurie Martin for advice on the title, which I took. Special thanks are due to my wife, Jeannie, who read the manuscript with great care and offered many helpful comments, together with our friends from a Zoom group in Charlottesville, Virginia, who devoted six months of weekly gatherings to discuss the book chapter by chapter. They are Erick and Deborah Birkett, Debby Clowney, David and Lois McKim, Dick and Janet Pearson, Deb Pruett, David and Doris Vander Meulen, and Elizabeth Vukman.

The influence of Old Testament scholar Derek Kidner (on my reading of the psalms) and professor C. S. Lewis (on my imagination) is evident throughout. Above all I must thank the late Edmund Clowney, mentor, teacher, and (for a time) fellow pastor. He long ago set my mind and imagination on the task of finding Christ in all the Scriptures. Sing Ed's hymn, "Who Shall Ascend the Mountain of the Lord" (292 in the *Trinity Hymnal*), and you will find moving expression of his Christ-loving devotional genius engaging Ps 24. He is not to be blamed if I have over-reached in my efforts here: the vision is his, but the exegesis is mine.

Introduction

Because I love all sorts of music, I find it impossible to identify any particular musical moment as my favorite. Nevertheless, there are some that stand out. One of them is Beethoven's rendering of the "Ode to Joy" at the beginning of the final movement of the *Ninth Symphony*. What makes it a favorite of mine is its richness. The melody I can easily hum, but there is no way I can reproduce from my own resources the harmony, counterpoint, and developing orchestration that unfold under Beethoven's hand.

Moments in sports can be just as difficult to reproduce. I have witnessed moments in World Cup soccer matches that were simply indescribable. The ablest sportswriter, let alone I, could never do them justice. The play, like Beethoven's music, was simply too grand; there was too much going on.

The psalms are, likewise, too full for our private consumption. This makes sense because they are not just "our songs for today." They are the songs of our fellow pilgrims over a long and rich communal history. They come to us from David, Solomon, Moses, Asaph, the sons of Korah, Heman, Ethan, and others whose names we do not know.[4] They were used in many ways and settings, not all of which are familiar to us—for private reflection and complaint, for pilgrimages, during the Passover, at royal inaugurations, in celebrations of deliverance both individual and corporate, at worship services, and during times of exile, flight, and misery.[5]

4. Seventy-three psalms are attributed in their titles to David, two to Solomon, twelve each to Asaph and to the sons of Korah (musicians of the temple choir founded under David), and one each to Moses, to Heman the Ezrahite (the founder of the sons of Korah), and to Ethan the Ezrahite (the founder of yet another choir). Kidner (*Psalms* 1–72, 32–36) gives us good cause for confidence in the authenticity of these titles, despite the objections of some scholars.

5. See Longman, *Psalms*, 19–35. He identifies seven types of psalms: Hymns (103),

Historian and Bible scholar N.T. Wright orients and challenges us:

> I'm not writing simply to say, "[The psalms] are important songs that we should use and try to understand." That is true, but it puts the emphasis the wrong way around, as though the psalms are the problem, and we should try to fit them into our world. Actually, again and again it is we, muddled and puzzled and half-believing, who are the problem; and the question is more how *we* can find our way into *their* world, into the faith and hope that shine out in one psalm after another . . . Not to try to inhabit them, while continuing to invent non-psalmic "worship" based on our own feelings of the moment, risks being like the spoiled child who, taken to the summit of Table Mountain with the city and the ocean spread out before him, refuses to gaze at the view because he is playing with his Game Boy.[6]

There is another reason why our experience does not always fully resonate with the psalms. The psalms contain yet another voice—that of Jesus, whose dedication, joy, and suffering far exceeded our own. When we read them, we encounter, to be sure, our own stories; but we encounter his story as well—the story of someone who loves God more fully than we do, who has travelled to deeper and darker places than we have, and who has triumphed far more than we ever could.[7]

We meet in him a person who put David's words into his own mouth because he chose to make David, Israel, and us his brothers and sisters experientially, to join us in the struggle to be human, and to succeed, for our good, where we fail. We could call the psalms Jesus' *hymnbook*, filled with words that he chose for our sake to recite and internalize during his time among us,[8] words that documented his chosen experience and gave expression to his faith, together with shape (and even necessity)[9] to his chosen destiny as our Savior and friend.

Laments (22), Thanks (18), Confidence (46), Remembrance (of the Exodus, 77; of the establishment of David's kingdom, 89, 132; of God's wonderful acts, 136), Wisdom (1), and Kingship (God's human king, 45; God as King, 98).

6. Wright, *Case*, 6.

7. See my preface.

8. Though the order, wording, and number of psalms Jesus had access to may be slightly different from what we presently have (Jesus may, for example, have made use of the Greek version of the Old Testament, while our book of Psalms is based on the Hebrew text), those variations were not substantial and make little difference for the purposes of this book.

9. Jesus spoke repeatedly of the "necessity" of his suffering and glory (see Matt 16:21,

To say that we get to meet Jesus in the psalms is not to suggest that we can simply, and without reflection or adjustment, import every word of every psalm into the mouth of Jesus, as if they perfectly captured his story, dreams, and struggles. Sometimes they have to be "tweaked" in the light of what we discover about him in the Gospels. And sometimes we encounter them more readily as our songs *to* or *about* him (Ps 45, which we discuss in chapter 2, is a good example of this) rather than his songs to God. Nevertheless, they all, in one way or another, bring us to Jesus.

In this book we are going to approach the psalms, for the most part, as Jesus' songs to God—as windows that open upon his heart and story as our fellow traveler.[10] As we do, you will discover (or discover more vividly) that you have a friend in high places (Emmanuel means "God with us") who knows what you face, who can help you make your way because he never caved in (see Heb 4:15–16), and who offered his lovely life as a perfect substitute for our less than lovely ones.

Think about it. Apart from the fact that Jesus never sinned, he was just like you. For your sake he was born into a family and grew up there, he asked questions because he did not know the answers to them, he needed friends and rejoiced in them, he was crushed by betrayal and loneliness, he longed for God and was tempted to disobey and mistrust him, he looked to God for wisdom, strength, protection, deliverance, comfort, and vindication, he yearned for justice, harmony, truth, and beauty, he got hungry and thirsty, and he suffered and died. There is no other place in the Bible where you get to see these realities more vividly than the psalms.

So let's plunge in. But before we do, may I offer some advice? Don't rush. Read one chapter on Sunday evening and then "camp out" every day the following week in the psalm(s) discussed in that chapter. Repeat the prayer at the end of the chapter each day. Or write prayers of your own. I suspect that you will find this practice very helpful.

Luke 24:26, etc.), a necessity that grew in his own mind as he engaged the Scriptures, including the Psalms (see Luke 24:44), as expressions of his own destiny.

10. Of course, Jesus is divine. But he is also fully human. It took the church over 450 years (at the Council of Chalcedon) to agree on a description of the nature of Christ—that he was one person with two natures, both fully human and fully divine "without being altered, disunited, or jumbled [i.e., confused]" (WCF, 8.2). This description explains nothing of the psychology of Jesus, but it does guard us from selling his humanity short in our worthy commitment to his deity. Reading the psalms as we are endeavoring to do makes that humanity vivid in a way that Chalcedon did not.

1

Putting David's Words into Jesus' Mouth

The Spirit of the Lord spoke by me; his word was on my tongue.

(2 Sam 23:2)

Jesus loved the psalms. Like you, perhaps, he grew up with them. No doubt he knew many of them by heart. N. T. Wright reports that "Jesus . . . would have known the psalms inside out."[1] In all likelihood he sang a number of them during and after the Last Supper.[2]

Strikingly, Jesus did not hesitate to quote David's words as if they were his own. Here is a sampling, the psalm portions in italics:

- Jesus foretold Judas's betrayal with words from Ps 41:9:

  > I am not speaking of all of you; I know whom I have chosen. But the Scripture will be fulfilled, "*He who ate my bread has lifted his heel against me.*" (John 13:18)

1. Wright, *Case*, 11.

2. See Matt 26:30: "And when they had sung a hymn, they went out to the Mount of Olives." The "hymn" here is likely one of the psalms from the "Egyptian Hallel" (Pss 113–118) routinely sung at the time of the Passover.

- As his anguish mounted during his dying hours, Jesus gave voice to Ps 22:1:

  > And at the ninth hour Jesus cried with a loud voice, *"Eloi, Eloi, lema sabachthani?" which means, "My God, my God, why have you forsaken me?"* (Mark 15:34)

- With his final breath Jesus gave himself to the Father using words from Ps 31:5:

  > Then Jesus, calling out with a loud voice, said, *"Father, into your hands I commit my spirit!"* And having said this he breathed his last. (Luke 23:46)

Noting what Jesus had done with the Psalms, the New Testament writers followed suit, routinely using David's own words to describe the deeds, attitudes, and experience of Jesus. Here is another sampling:

- Peter ascribes words to Jesus from Ps 16:8–11 during his Pentecost sermon:

  > For David says concerning him,
  > *I saw the Lord always before me,*
  > *for he is at my right hand that I may not be shaken;*
  > *therefore my heart was glad, and my tongue rejoiced;*
  > *my flesh also will dwell in hope.*
  > *For you will not abandon my soul to Hades,*
  > *or let your Holy One see corruption.*
  > *You have made known to me the paths of life;*
  > *you will make me full of gladness with your presence.*
  > (Acts 2:25–28)

- John explains Jesus' cleansing of the temple with words from Ps 69:9:

  > And he told those who sold the pigeons, "Take these things away; do not make my Father's house a house of trade." His disciples remembered that it was written, *"Zeal for your house will consume me."* (John 2:16–17)

- Paul urges stronger Christians to be patient with weaker ones in imitation of Christ, whose readiness to endure unfair rebukes finds expression in Ps 69:9:

> We who are strong have an obligation to bear with the failings of the weak, and not to please ourselves. Let each of us please his neighbor for his good, to build him up. For Christ did not please himself, but as it is written, "*The reproaches of those who reproached you fell on me.*" (Rom 15:1–3)

- The writer of Hebrews puts words from Ps 22:22 into the crucified and resurrected Jesus' mouth:

> For it was fitting that God, for whom and by whom all things exist, in bringing many sons to glory, should make the founder of their salvation [Jesus] perfect through suffering. For he who sanctifies and those who are sanctified all have one source. That is why he is not ashamed to call them brothers, saying,
> "*I will tell your name to my brothers;*
> *in the midst of the congregation I will sing your praise.*"
> (Heb 2:10–12)

- Hebrews invites us to hear Jesus dedicating his life and body to the Father in the words of Ps 40:6–8:

> Consequently, when Christ came into the world, he said,
> "*Sacrifices and offerings you have not desired,*
> *but a body have you prepared for me;*
> *in burnt offerings and sin offerings*
> *you have taken no pleasure.*
> *Then I said, 'Behold, I have come to do your will, O God,*
> *as it is written of me in the scroll of the book.*'"
> (Heb 10:5–7)

HOW CAN THEY DO THIS WITH DAVID'S WORDS?

Think about it. Ancient words and attitudes, spoken and experienced as many as a thousand years before Jesus appeared on the scene, are simply lifted from the mouths and lives of those who lived them and dropped onto Jesus. David's rescue from death becomes Jesus'. Likewise, David's zeal for God's honor, his suffering, and his testimony to his friends after God has rescued him become Jesus'.

This seems like quite a stretch, a bit like someone asserting that Augustine's *Confessions* are really Pope Francis'. I suppose we could say that the Pope's confessions are *like* Augustine's (or, better, like St. Francis of Assisi's, since the two men share common experiences and concerns). But the New

Testament writers, and Jesus himself, are saying something stronger: that the words of David *are*, without ceasing to be David's words, the words of the Messiah, that they are in a mysterious sense more fully his than they were David's. They seem to be saying that there is a deeper meaning embedded in David's experience than David himself knew—that David's story anticipated Jesus' story.

Peter makes this very point in his Pentecost sermon, quoting from Ps 16:10:

> *For you will not abandon my soul to Hades,*
> *or let your Holy One see corruption . . .*
> Brothers, I may say to you with confidence about the patriarch David that he both died and was buried, and his tomb is with us to this day. Being therefore a prophet, and knowing that God had sworn with an oath to him that he would set one of his descendants on his throne, he foresaw and spoke about the resurrection of the Christ, that he was not abandoned to Hades, nor did his flesh see corruption. This Jesus God raised up, and of that we all are witnesses. (Acts 2:27, 29–32).

Peter says, in effect, "How can 'you will not abandon my soul to Hades' be David's words when we all know that his bones are buried right here in Jerusalem. He had to be speaking of someone other than himself, even as he spoke of himself."

This is not to say that David's experience (or any other psalmist's) did not stand on its own, that the Psalms did not have rich meaning in their own settings. Of course they did, and we miss their richness if we simply try to make them point to Jesus and his story. But we also miss their richness if we stop with David. Not even David stopped with David, declaring in one of his final utterances, "The Spirit of the Lord speaks by me; his word is on my tongue" (2 Sam 23:2). God had promised a Messiah long before the first psalm was written, and it should not surprise us that the Spirit of God would choose to give voice to that Messiah throughout the sacred texts that anticipated him, including the Psalms.

Later, Peter explains what was going on as the prophets (David among them)[3] wrote:

> Concerning this salvation, the prophets who prophesied about the grace that was to be yours searched and inquired carefully, inquiring what person or time the Spirit of Christ in them was indicating

3. See Acts 2:30 where, in his Pentecost message, Peter describes David as "a prophet."

> when he predicted the sufferings of Christ and the subsequent glories. (1 Pet 1:10–11)

We hear the voice of the Messiah in the Psalms because the Spirit of the Messiah was in the psalmists.

THE DEEPER SONG

Let me put things this way. There has always been a deeper story embedded in the particular stories of God's people (including his psalmists), the story known to God but only partially known to them. The story goes back to the garden of Eden, when, after Adam and Eve had turned from God, God promised to come to us as one of us (the "offspring" of Eve) and destroy, through his own suffering, the darkness we have brought upon ourselves.[4] It is a story so old that it was known in heaven before the world began:

> You were ransomed from the futile ways inherited from your forefathers, not with perishable things such as silver or gold, but with the precious blood of Christ, like that of a lamb without blemish or spot. He was foreknown before the foundation of the world but was made manifest in the last times for . . . [your] sake. (1 Pet 1:18–20)

This deeper story, a story God loves to tell, keeps popping up in the psalms. It surfaces very personally, because the psalms are very personal, as Eve's spiritual children (the people of God represented by David and the other psalmists) keep anticipating in their experiences of suffering and deliverance the day when her greatest descendent will endure the ultimate suffering and enjoy the ultimate deliverance.

What I am saying is that the psalms have always been the songs of the Messiah, coming to us through the lives and experiences of the psalmists. Consider what this means. It means that you will find Jesus' story—his heart, his struggles, his joys, his pain and deliverance—"hidden" in the psalms—not just in one or two obviously messianic psalms but in all of them. It means, therefore, that you will miss out on the fullness of the psalms if you read them as if they were just about you, or about David and his fellow psalmists.

Of course you will, and should, read the psalms as your own songs, as David's songs, and as the songs of ancient Israel. But you must not stop

4. See Gen 3:15.

there. If you do, you will miss seeing Jesus—and that means that you will miss their deepest purpose and your deepest hope.

The following prayer may help you engage more fully in what I have been saying. Similar prayers will appear at the end of every chapter.

Lord Jesus, you are more than my brother, but you are not less. When I hear your voice in the Psalms, I discover that you know my experience from the inside. You know what it feels like to be betrayed by friends and abandoned by God, to be burnt out with loving people and to be grieved by what's wrong with the world. You know how it feels to be blamed for things you did not do and to grieve with brothers and sisters over great loss. You know what it feels like to have to trust God when everything is collapsing around you, when you have to wait on him to come through because there is nothing else to be done. You know what it feels like to delight with friends when God does something amazing. You know what it feels like to die and to be raised from death. You know what it feels like to tell your dearest friends, friends like me, that we don't have to perish eternally, thanks to what you have done. Lord Jesus, you did not have to enter my story, but you did because you love me and wanted to bring me safely home with you to the Father. I love you for this. Amen.

2

A Leader Worth Loving

Psalm 45

My heart overflows with a pleasing theme; I address my verses to the king.
(Ps 45:1)

We are aiming in this book to hear the voice *of* Jesus in the psalms. But before we give ourselves fully to that task, I want to note that we sing many of the psalms *to* Jesus. As Edmund Clowney, one of my favorite teachers and mentors, often taught, Jesus is both the Servant of the covenant and the Lord of the covenant—he occupies both sides of the "God-man" relationship. It should not surprise us, then, that we discover him in both of these roles in the songs God has given us.

ROYAL WEDDING SONG

Psalm 45 is one of the most stirring tributes to Jesus in the Psalter. Read it aloud:

> My heart overflows with a pleasing theme;
> I address my verses to the king;
> my tongue is like the pen of a ready scribe.

You are the most handsome of the sons of men;
grace is poured upon your lips;
therefore God has blessed you forever.
Gird your sword on your thigh, O mighty one,
in your splendor and majesty!

In your majesty ride out victoriously
for the cause of truth and meekness and righteousness;
let your right hand teach you awesome deeds!
Your arrows are sharp
in the heart of the king's enemies;
the peoples fall under you.

Your throne, O God, is forever and ever.
The scepter of your kingdom is a scepter of uprightness;
you have loved righteousness and hated wickedness.
Therefore God, your God, has anointed you
with the oil of gladness beyond your companions;
your robes are all fragrant with myrrh and aloes and cassia.
From ivory palaces stringed instruments make you glad;
daughters of kings are among your ladies of honor;
at your right hand stands the queen in gold of Ophir.

Hear, O daughter, and consider, and incline your ear:
forget your people and your father's house,
and the king will desire your beauty.
Since he is your lord, bow to him.
The people of Tyre will seek your favor with gifts,
the richest of the people.

All glorious is the princess in her chamber, with robes interwoven with gold.
In many-colored robes she is led to the king,
with her virgin companions following behind her.
With joy and gladness they are led along
as they enter the palace of the king.

In place of your fathers shall be your sons;
you will make them princes in all the earth.
I will cause your name to be remembered in all generations;
therefore nations will praise you forever and ever.
(Ps 45:1–17)

We have here a song composed for a royal wedding and arising from the eager imagination of a songwriter whose heart "overflows." Everything that we associate with a really good wedding is here: family and friends, change, joy and laughter, elegant clothing and pageantry, pleasing smells and good music, sexual passion, goodness, love, and devotion. And overlaying all of these stirring elements there is the joy that we associate in our culture with the victory celebration when our presidential candidate wins. For the union the psalmist sings about is between a king and his beloved, promising not only joyful intimacy between the two but lasting peace and justice for the nation and, beyond that, for the world.

THE ROYAL GROOM

At the center of this hope is the mysterious figure of the royal groom (his anonymity suggests that he is an ideal, somehow more than a man). We sing *to* him, not simply *about* him ("You are," not "He is") in terms that come close to worship. He is surpassingly handsome—"the most handsome of the sons of men" (Ps 45:2). This does not mean he is "photoshoot hot"—like a movie star. It means that he is profoundly attractive, a public figure who draws forth our heart-felt allegiance.

What gives him such charisma is his character. First there are his words: "Grace is poured upon your lips" (Ps 45:2). We grow weary of public figures who lie, grandstand, demean, and misinform. This king is so different: his mouth is like a desert oasis. Talk with him for five minutes—or just overhear him speaking—and you come away refreshed, hopeful, up-built. Luke would later write, "All spoke well of [Jesus] and marveled at the gracious words that were coming from his mouth" (Luke 4:22).

Matching the grace of the king's speech is the nobility of his character:

> In your majesty ride out victoriously
> for the cause of truth, meekness, and righteousness . . .
> You have loved righteousness and hated wickedness.
> (Ps 45:4, 7)

The king is a good man, deeply so. As a rule, the closer we get to each other, the more flaws we see. But with this person it is different. The closer we get to him the better he looks—which is one of the reasons his bride to be is so genuinely dazzled by him. He champions the right, neither to score political points nor to win a woman's heart but because he genuinely loves what is right and genuinely hates what is not.

HUMBLE AND GOOD

A striking feature in this king's goodness is that it is both meek and righteous (see Ps 45:4). These two words actually translate a single hyphenated Hebrew word, meaning that his goodness and his humility arise with equal force in him. Many of the good people we know are often off-putting because a critical spirit comes with the goodness. Many of the humble people we know can frustrate us because they seem to have no standards. But this king is both: he is utterly accessible and kind and, at the same time, utterly firm when it comes to what is right and true.

It's as if the psalmist had read the Gospels, for this is the person we find there. Jesus was meek: he loved unlovely people; he never seized power, not when the mobs tried to make him king by force, nor when his enemies dressed him in scarlet and laughed at him. But Jesus was also unflinching when it came to loving God and us: he spoke always and only the truth, even when it infuriated his enemies; he always and only did what was right, even when it meant turning toward Jerusalem over the protests of Peter. When Jesus grieved over Jerusalem, he did so both in sorrow over the coming judgment and in affirmation of it.[1]

Jesus surprises us with a character that does not fit our expectations: He is neither a progressive nor a traditionalist. He delivers the adulteress from her accusers and then says to her, "Go, and . . . sin no more" (John 8:11).

CHAMPION

One more quality shines in the royal groom of the psalm. His goodness vanquishes every foe:

> In your majesty ride out victoriously
> for the cause of truth and meekness and righteousness;
> let your right hand teach you awesome deeds.
> Your arrows are sharp
> in the king's enemies;
> the peoples fall under you. (Ps 45:4–5)

1. See John 6:15, Matt 27:28–31, Mark 14:60–65, Matt 16:21–23, and Matt 23:37–38.

Here is a leader to love and trust. He is a winner in the battles that matter. Like David before Goliath he stands up to arrogance and wickedness and throws them down.

To follow such a leader is to move your life in the right direction. It is to know that you will be treated with respect and fairness by the one you follow. It is to know that your love for what is right and true will be appreciated by him, even if no one else appreciates it. And because he is going to win, you will be vindicated: he loves you as this king loves his bride and fully intends to share his triumph with you.

GRACIOUS IN TRIUMPH

One of the many moving moments in *The Lord of the Rings* occurs when Sam and Frodo, newly awakened after their ordeal at Mount Doom, find themselves, against all hope, alive and with their friend Gandalf, the great wizard who has guided them in their quest. He invites them to don the rags that they wore in Mordor and to follow him to meet the newly triumphant King Aragorn. Here is what follows:

> As they came to the opening in the wood, they were surprised to see knights in bright mail and tall guards in silver and black standing there, who greeted them with honor and bowed before them . . .
>
> The red blood blushing in their faces and their eyes shining with wonder, Frodo and Sam went forward and saw that amidst the clamorous host were set three high-seats built on green turves . . . On the [highest] throne sat a mail-clad man, a great sword laid across his knees . . . As they drew near he rose. And then they knew him, changed as he was, so high and glad of face, kingly, lord of Men, dark-haired with eyes of grey . . .
>
> And then to Sam's surprise and utter confusion [the king] bowed his knee before them; and taking them by the hand, Frodo upon his right hand and Sam upon his left, he led them to the throne, and setting them upon it, he turned to the men and captains who stood by and spoke, so that his voice rang over all the host, crying:
>
> "Praise them with great praise!"[2]

2. Tolkien, *Return*, 231–32.

In Sam and Frodo's story, theirs was the darkest road. In the Bible's story that road belonged to the king himself. But in both stories, the real king wins, and in victory he remembers you and me—rising to greet and honor us. We who "suffer with him . . . [will] also be glorified with him" (Rom 8:17).

LOVING THE KING

Such a king is worth leaving everything to follow:

> Hear, O daughter, and consider, and incline your ear:
> forget your people and your father's house,
> and the king will desire your beauty.
> Since he is your lord, bow to him. (Ps 45:10–11)

These are difficult words to hear in an egalitarian age, doubly difficult when we know so many stories of abuse. But the psalm invites you and me to look past our broken experiences with each other to a non-abusive arrangement, one in which glory and honor are freely shared, one in which love and desire meet, one in which the outcome of the union promises great goodness extending to all the earth and on into eternity.

We know this because in the midst of extolling the *human* king ("In your majesty ride out victoriously . . . your arrows are sharp . . . Your God has anointed you" [Ps 45:4, 5, 7]) the poet abruptly cries,

> "Your throne, *O God*, is forever and ever" (Ps 45:6).

It is as if, for a moment, the curtain parts and we see through the human king to the divine one. The deeper story that we mentioned in chapter one asserts itself.

In this psalm, as in many of the royal psalms,[3] we find ourselves at what N. T. Wright calls a "crossroads of time."[4] We look with delight upon a present, if idealized, royal wedding while simultaneously looking with hope at the day when God himself will come with great goodness and love to take the nations as his bride.

3. So called because they celebrate in part or in the whole the enthronement or rule of God's king: Pss 2, 18, 20, 21, 45, etc.

4. Wright, *Case*, 20. Ps 89, for example, looks back to God's original covenant with David and forward to the everlasting triumph of David's son, while bemoaning God's present rejection of David's line (see Wright, *Case*, 67–73).

So the king is not just an idealized human figure. He is also God with us, whose name the psalmist did not know—but we do. And the bride is more than an anonymous figure from antiquity. She is you and I, made lovely by the king's love. The king who desires her is a picture of the king who desires us and has come to find and redeem us at immeasurable cost to himself:

> Christ loved the church and gave himself up for her, that he might sanctify her, having cleansed her by the washing of water with the word, so that he might present the church to himself in splendor, without spot or wrinkle or any such thing, that she might be holy and without blemish. (Eph 5:25–27)

We get to "bow to him" (Ps 45:11) with gratitude and wonder.

HAPPILY EVER AFTER

Think of all those moments in great love stories when it dawns on someone that the other person, the one who has seemed so unreachable and uninterested, actually loves him or her deeply. Now hear in those moments a whisper from God, an invitation to catch a glimpse of his surprising and undeserved longings for you. You must not trivialize God's love by turning him into your boyfriend. But neither should you turn a blind eye to the noble passion you find in Ps 45 and assume that it tells you nothing about God.

A medieval poet asks us to imagine Christ on the eve of his Second Coming:

> Tomorrow shall be my dancing day:
> I would my true love did so chance
> To see the legend of my play,
> To call my true love to my dance:
> Sing O, my love, my love;
> This have I done for my true love.[5]

You are desired.

Lord Jesus, there is no one like you. No human being has every wielded power the way you do. Every word you utter is gracious. Every deed is true, humble, and kind. There is nothing performative about you: you genuinely love what is right and hate what is wicked; you fully measure

5. Willcocks and Rutter, "Tomorrow," 350–56.

the heart; you defend the weak, heal the sick, and feed the poor because you love to serve those you rule. Most astounding, you actually desire us, seeking our company and conversation.

I confess that I find it almost impossible to believe that you are really like this. Forgive my doubt and the behavior that flows from it. I do not reflect you very well: what power I have I tend to use for myself; I am slow to serve; I am quick to evaluate people by their appearance; I often ignore those whom I am in a position to help.

What hope it gives me to know that you have triumphed over sin and death, for I never could. It is only a matter of time before you crush every sorrow, sin, and injustice under your feet. And when you do, you will not be content to be alone in your triumph. You intend gladly to share it with us, for we are your bride. We are, even now, decked out in your own moral beauty, and will one day reflect that beauty fully from the inside out. How good it is to be so deeply loved. Amen.

3

Sharing Our Story

Psalm 90

Make us glad for as many days as you have afflicted us, and for as many years as we have seen evil. Let your work be shown to your servants, and your glorious power to their children.

(Ps 90:15–16)

THE PSALTER IS FULL of "we" songs—corporate expressions of faith, lament, and praise:

> Lord, you have been our dwelling place
> in all generations. (Ps 90:1)

> When the LORD restored the fortunes of Zion,
> we were like those who dream.
> Then our mouth was filled with laughter,
> and our tongue with shouts of joy;
> then they said among the nations,
> "The LORD has done great things for them."
> The LORD has done great things for us;
> we are glad. (Ps 126:1–3)

> O God, why do you cast us off forever?
> Why does your anger smoke against the sheep of your pasture?
> (Ps 74:1)

All of these "we" passages remind us of our solidarity with other believers down the ages and across cultures.

They also remind us of our solidarity with Jesus, for he received them as his own. Stop for a moment and imagine Jesus sighing, "O God, why do you cast us off forever," alongside you. Do this with any of the scores of "we" songs that we find in the psalms. If you do, it will open your eyes to his love in new ways. You will feel more acutely the wonder of what John meant when he said, "And the Word became flesh and dwelt among us" (John 1:14).

READING PS 90 WITH JESUS

One "we" song is Ps 90. Read it aloud and imagine Jesus reading it alongside you. Listen for his voice:

> Lord, you have been our dwelling place
> in all generations.
> Before the mountains were brought forth,
> or ever you had formed the earth and the world,
> from everlasting to everlasting you are God.
>
> You return man to dust
> and say, "Return, O children of man!"
> For a thousand years in your sight
> are but as yesterday when it is past,
> or as a watch in the night.
>
> You sweep them away as with a flood; they are like a dream,
> like grass that is renewed in the morning:
> in the morning it flourishes and is renewed;
> in the evening it fades and withers.
>
> For we are brought to an end by your anger;
> by your wrath we are dismayed.
> You have set our iniquities before you,
> our secret sins in the light of your presence.
>
> For all our days pass away under your wrath;
> we bring our years to an end like a sigh.
> The years of our life are seventy,
> or even by reason of strength eighty;

yet their span is but toil and trouble;
    they are soon gone, and we fly away.
Who considers the power of your anger,
    and your wrath according to the fear of you?

So teach us to number our days
    that we may get a heart of wisdom.
Return, O LORD! How long?
    Have pity on your servants!
Satisfy us in the morning with your steadfast love,
    that we may rejoice and be glad all our days.
Make us glad for as many days as you have afflicted us,
    and for as many years as we have seen evil.
Let your work be shown to your servants,
    and your glorious power to their children.
Let the favor of the Lord our God be upon us,
    and establish the work of our hands upon us;
    yes, establish the work of our hands! (Ps 90:1–17)

A Song Chosen by Jesus

This is a searching and somber song about our shared mortality, attributed to Moses, a man who had lived long and endured much before he wrote it. It is also a song that Jesus knew and chose fully to embrace.

Jesus had to learn from childhood, when living in Egyptian exile, to call God his only true "dwelling place" (Ps 90:1). Though he deserved no wrath, he nevertheless chose to live all his days under the shadow of God's wrath (see Ps 90:7–9), feeling our world's unhappy distance from God, as we all do. Knowing that his "days" were few, he prayed, as we do, for the wisdom to "number" them (Ps 90:12). Living, as we all do, in the midst of "toil and trouble" (Ps 90:10), he prayed, as we all must, for favor to "establish the work of [his] hands" (Ps 90:17). He prayed, as we all do, for gladness and relief from the power of evil. His life was frail and uncertain, subject to the whim of Augustus, who forced his mother to travel while pregnant with him from Nazareth to Bethlehem, subject to the callousness of Pilate and the brutality of his soldiers. He saw and felt what was wrong with the world and cried out, as we all sometimes do, "Return, O Lord! How long? Have pity on your servants!" (Ps 90:13).

A SONG REPEATEDLY CHOSEN BY JESUS

Jesus' chosen solidarity with you and me wasn't occasional, only at crisis moments, but continual. Psalm 90, in other words, was his song every day of his life.

At his arrest in the garden of Gethsemane, Jesus told Peter not to rise in his defense: "Do you think that I cannot appeal to my Father, and he will at once send me more than twelve legions of angels?" (Matt 26:53). This choice, made at the end of Jesus' life, parallels the choice Jesus made at the beginning of his public ministry not to turn stones into bread. It tells us that the Son of God's decision to join us in our human story was a decision he kept making.

Some of us occasionally have the power to deliver ourselves from the frailties, uncertainties, and trials that trouble us—say, through good medical care, or wise counsel, or adequate income. Jesus always had that power, even as he hung on the cross and his tormentors mockingly urged him to use it. But he never did.

Jesus never, in other words, took an end-run around Ps 90. He allowed himself to be taken, without relief, to the farthest reaches of the dark side of human experience—all the way to execution and the full "power of [God's] anger and wrath" (Ps 90:11). And the reason he submitted to this was so that, when he came to the place of execution as our substitute, what he could offer there was a fully, rather than a partly, human life—a life just like yours. He was tempted "*in every respect . . . as we are*, yet without sin" (Heb 4:15).

A SONG CHOSEN FOR US

Jesus' repeatedly chosen solidarity with us has brought us two incomparable benefits if we belong to him. It has brought us a powerful friend, one who is fully able "to sympathize with [us in] our weaknesses" (Heb 4:15). Whatever difficulty you may be going through you can talk to him about it with the confidence that he knows what you are experiencing from the inside and can help you manage it.

And Jesus brings you and me more than coping skills (this is the second benefit). His solidarity with us will, in the end, deliver us completely. His choice fully to share human life with us will bring us completely out from under every sin and trauma, even death itself, because that life was, unlike ours, perfectly obedient (he was "tempted as we are, *yet without sin*" [Heb 4:15]), and Jesus offered it in substitution for ours. Jesus knows better than you or I will ever know (or need to know) the answer to the question, "Who considers the power of your anger, and your wrath according to the fear of you?" (Ps 90:11), because he bore that wrath so that we could escape it.

FEELING THE INCARNATION THROUGH THE PSALMS

Reading the "we" psalms with Jesus will make his love and empathy more vivid to you. It will increase your love for and confidence in him.

Here is a practical suggestion. The next time you read a "we" psalm (any psalm, actually), read it aloud. And as you hear your voice, imagine that it is the voice of Jesus reciting those words when he lived among us. Hear him doing with those words what you, his younger brother or sister, are trying to do with them. Imagine him internalizing them, making them his own. Imagine him using those words to give him the language to express, and to trust God in the midst of, the life he has chosen to share with you. Imagine Jesus meditating on those words as he says them, allowing them to give shape to his calling and destiny, a calling and destiny that will take him to darker places than you will ever have to go to, and then into a deliverance into which he will carry you. Imagine him, finally, thinking about you as he recites those words alongside you now, glad to be your brother, your fellow pilgrim, and your deliverer.

Follow this suggestion, and you will not only meet Jesus in that psalm. You will likely be moved and changed by the encounter.

Blessed Redeemer, you know everything about me, but you were not content to know me from a distance. You chose instead to enter my story fully. Though you were the Creator, you chose to learn from childhood to call God, rather than anything temporal, your home. Though you deserved no wrath, you nevertheless lived under the shadow of God's wrath, feeling the weight of it, as I sometimes do. Knowing that your days were numbered, you prayed, as I should, for the wisdom to make them count. Living fully, as I do, in the midst of toil and trouble, you prayed, as I ought to, for favor to establish the work of your hands. You prayed, as I often do, for gladness and relief from the power of evil. Your life was frail and uncertain, subject to the whim of human authority, crushed in the end by merciless brutality, a failed life by every human measure.

Though you could at any time have withdrawn from human life as I know it, or made it less difficult, you never did. Through it all you kept singing my songs alongside me, making them your own expressions of trust, joy, and despair. Not even in your final hours, as you cried out from hell, did you deny the Father. You did all this so that at the end you could offer your life in place of mine, a lovely gown of daily obedience in place of my rags of tepid and broken trust. Thank you for fulfilling all righteousness on my behalf. Thank you for walking with me into the darkest places and beyond. Amen.

4

A Life That Counts

Psalm 1

Blessed is the man . . . [whose] delight is in the law of the LORD . . . In all that he does he prospers.

(Ps 1:1, 2, 3)

I REMEMBER A YOUNG mother with two daughters—one of whom was very talented at drawing, the other less so. On one memorable occasion an adult friend of the family happened upon the two girls as they were busy sketching. She noticed the less talented daughter's work first and said, "That's very nice." But she then noticed the other child's work and declared, "This is amazing!" and reached over to take a closer look. The mother watched with pain and sadness as the younger child quickly pulled her work from public view and withdrew into herself.

We all want our lives to count. We want to make a valuable contribution to the world and the people around us—and we want to be noticed for that contribution. We often make a mess of this desire, giving it twisted expression in a range of forms: envy, selfish ambition, and sullen withdrawal are three that I can think of. But this desire is at root legitimate. It is built in and God given.

LIVES THAT GOD LOVES TO RECOGNIZE

Psalm 1, the "faithful doorkeeper"[1] to the Psalter, assures us of God's high expectations for us. Take a moment to read it aloud:

> Blessed is the man
> who walks not in the counsel of the wicked,
> nor stands in the way of sinners,
>   nor sits in the seat of scoffers;
> but his delight is in the law of the LORD,
>   and on his law he meditates day and night.
>
> He is like a tree
>   planted by streams of water
> that yields its fruit in its season,
>   and its leaf does not wither.
> In all that he does, he prospers.
> The wicked are not so,
>   but are like chaff that the wind drives away.
>
> Therefore the wicked will not stand in the judgment,
>   nor sinners in the congregation of the righteous;
> for the LORD knows the way of the righteous,
>   but the way of the wicked will perish. (Ps 1:1–6)

Like the mother in the story, God wants you to be "like a tree planted by streams of water that yields its fruit in its season, and [whose] leaves do not wither" (Ps 1:3). God wants you to be as good at being a person as well-watered trees are at being trees, so that lovely things, of benefit to others, things that please him, issue from your life.

God does not want your life to turn to dust, blowing away "like chaff" during the winnowing process (Ps 1:4).[2] He rather wants you to "prosper" in "all" that you do (Ps 1:3). You may need to be patient (fruit comes "in season"), but God gave you this psalm to assure you that he intends for you to have a "weighty" life—not necessarily problem free (Joseph was faithful and look where it got him!) but a life worth having lived—"known [recognized and delighted over]" by the LORD (Ps 1:6).

1. Kidner, *Psalms 1–72*, 47.

2. In winnowing, the harvester tosses the good wheat and its useless outer husk (chaff) upward into the wind. The wind blows the weightless chaff away while permitting the more substantive grain to fall to the ground where it is gathered up and put to good use.

HOW DO WE BUILD LIVES THAT COUNT?

We are already valuable (God made us in his image, after all). But we don't always live up to it. Psalm 1 shows us how. We don't do so by competing with other people, as the child does in the story I just told. Nor do we do so by becoming well-known, or hanging out with the right people, or accumulating things, or withdrawing into solitude and contemplation, or being true to ourselves (an elusive quest since it is often impossible to figure ourselves out).

We live lives that count, according to Ps 1, by "delighting in the law of the Lord" (Ps 1:2). "Law" ("Torah" in Hebrew) means instruction and includes the full range of what we find in the Scriptures: not just God's commands but his story, his promises and presence, his account of us and himself, his advice and wisdom, his delights and character. And this law we are to "delight in" (not just know), "meditat[ing]" on it [chewing on it] "day and night" (Ps 1:2).

JUST SAY NO

Such delighting will involve repeatedly saying "no" to certain things:

> Blessed is the man
> who walks not in the counsel of the wicked,
> nor stands in the way of sinners,
>   nor sits in the seat of scoffers. (Ps 1:1)

Does this mean that you and I are supposed to be snobs, huffily searching the landscape for the "bad guys" so that we can make a point of having nothing to do with them? It can't mean this, given what the God of Torah is like. He comes in search of Adam after he disobeyed,[3] he "sends rain on the just and on the unjust," he keeps close company with the consciences of every person (his word "gives light to everyone"), and he actively gives life and breath to all ("in him we live and move and have our being"),[4] even those who use that life to do terrible things.

Think about Jesus. He is just like his Father—welcoming people without becoming like them. As his public ministry begins he identifies with us in baptism over John's objections. At the end he promises to receive the

3. See Gen 3:8–21.

4. Matt 5:45, John 1:9, and Acts 17:28.

repentant thief into Paradise. And along the way he routinely "hangs out" with disreputable people like Zacchaeus, the tax collector.[5] And Jesus is still like this, welcoming us even during our very dark seasons and in the midst of our very selfish choices.

We "delight in the law of the Lord," then, by emulating Jesus, who himself emulates the Father. We don't avoid people, but we do resist whatever godless attitudes and ways of thinking people tend to bring to life. We befriend, for example, those who ignore or defy God (the "wicked"), but we don't allow their "counsel" (their advice on how to solve problems or to perceive reality or to deal with people) to direct our behavior. We hang out with those who choose to ignore God's law ("sinners"), but we don't do what they do. We live and work with "scoffers," cynical friends who deny that goodness can be found or its Source known, but we don't channel ("sit in the seat of") their darkness.

A PORTRAIT OF OUR REDEEMER

Psalm 1 is the North Star for the beautiful and memorable life. It makes vivid how to find our way to true flourishing. But it also discourages us if we take it to heart because the pressures on us to take the wrong path (the path of "the wicked") are often too strong. What helps enormously is discovering that God has given us Ps 1 only secondarily as a roadmap for us. His chief intent is to give us a portrait of his beloved Son, whom he has sent to make us beautiful and to bring us safely home.

Think again about Jesus. We have just noted how richly he lived out verse 1. We see him as well in verse 2, "delighting in the Law" of God as he astonishes the temple scholars with his questions as a boy.[6] Later in life, Jesus' ready biblical answers to every satanic assault in the wilderness show him to be one who has for years "meditate[d] day and night" on God's word. When Jesus declares, "Man shall not live by bread alone but by every word that comes from the mouth of God" (Matt 4:4), he describes his own profound and life-long dependence on Torah.

Such beauty we do not yet display. But we will one day, thanks to Jesus.

5. See Matt 3:13–15, Luke 23:39–43, Luke 19:1–10.

6. See Luke 2:41–51.

A TEAR IN THE PORTRAIT

There is a troubling tear in the portrait we have just described. We see it when we think of Jesus' suffering. Prior to his final hours, the promised outcomes of the good life filled his story. He "prosper[ed]" in "all" that he did: his words drew vast crowds and confounded his enemies, he healed hundreds and fed the multitudes, he cast out demons and commanded the wind and waters of Galilee. His Father "knew" him (Ps 1:6), delighting in him: "You are my beloved son; with you I am well pleased" (Mark 1:11).

But then everything fell apart. The man who refused to "walk . . . in the counsel of the wicked" was condemned by wicked men and crucified as a wicked man in the company of wicked men. The man who refused to scoff at his enemies, was mercilessly scoffed by them: they dressed him up as a king, pressed a crown of thorns down upon his head, and bowed before him in mock worship; they blindfolded and struck him brutally; they spat on him; they beat him mercilessly; they stripped off his clothes; they killed him.[7]

And all of this cruelty wasn't the worst of it. As Jesus hung nailed to a cross in obedience to his Father's instruction, his Father blew him off "like chaff." God didn't "know" him: he ignored him, forgot him, left him to the cruelty of wicked people.

Have you ever found yourself crying out in perplexity, "Lord, I have sought you in this thing—so why am I having such a hard time?" Times like this can be very difficult, but the disjunction we may feel is small compared to what it was for Jesus—for even at our best moments our lives are flawed and self-centered. We never perfectly measure up to verses 1–2. But Jesus did.

WHY DID PS 1 NOT "WORK" FOR JESUS?

Why did the moral world of Ps 1 fall apart for Jesus at the end of his life? Because at that dark moment, Jesus chose the outcome that otherwise should have come to us.

Try a thought experiment. Imagine Jesus reflecting on verses 4–6 with you and me in mind:

> The wicked are
> . . . like chaff that the wind drives away.
> Therefore the wicked will not stand in the judgment,

7. See Mark 14: 65, 15:16–32, and parallels.

> nor sinners in the congregation of the righteous;
> . . . the way of the wicked will perish. (Ps 1:4–5, 6)

Do you hear Jesus smugly saying, "Glad I'm not one of them!" Or don't you rather hear him pleading for you:

> Father, I don't want this to happen to him. I don't want her to be forgotten. I don't want them to perish. I don't want their lives to go up in smoke! What can I do, what must I do, to make sure that they will be able to stand in the judgment?

We don't know precisely when in his earthly life Jesus learned the answer to this question. He certainly knew it by the time that he told his disciples that he had to go to Jerusalem and die.[8] He knew that he had to swap lives with us, so that the life and destiny of the wicked would be his rather than ours and the life and destiny of the Torah lover would be ours rather than his. And this is what he did. He lived in our place the morally beautiful and fruitful life set forth in the psalm, the life that we should live but as yet do not. And then, at the end, as he passed his lovely legacy on to us, he took our dark legacy upon himself. He became chaff so that we could become fruit-bearing and beloved trees in his Father's garden.

A NEW AND LOVELY DESTINY FOR US

What a relief it is to read verses 1–2 and to know that there exists a fellow traveler (our substitute, our friend and brother) who lived those words to God's fullest satisfaction—to know that his life counted, not just for his sake but for ours. What a relief to know that, though our lives are so deeply compromised and tarnished by our crimes, we can be fully rehabilitated in Jesus—forgiven, restored and mended into a great beauty.

Seeing and believing this story will do something mysterious and deeply satisfying inside you. It will encourage you so profoundly that you actually begin to change. You will find verses 1–2 becoming increasingly descriptive of you. You will find your delight in God and his instruction growing. You will find your life prospering more than it otherwise might have. You will find your awareness of your value deepening. You will find your confidence rising that God knows and delights in you now and that he

8. See Matt 16:21: "Jesus began to show his disciples that he must go to Jerusalem . . . and be killed."

will remember and honor you when you meet him face-to-face when all is said and done. How encouraging. How motivating.

Like a loving parent, Lord, you want my life to count. You mean for me to prosper in every good way, just like you did when you walked among us. You want me to delight in God's wisdom so deeply that it comes to rich expression in all that I say and do. You want these good things so that, at the end of my days, you will with glad recognition call my name and welcome me home.

You desire these good things for me so earnestly that you joined me in my humanity in order to trade your life and destiny with mine— living out the life I ought to live but don't, and then perishing in my place so that I wouldn't have to. At the end of your days you became like chaff, blown away by people who despised you, abandoned by God, so that I would never be disowned.

There is no way I can adequately thank you for what you have done. Please Lord, fill me with yourself, write your law on my heart, and wean me from sin and cynicism. I love you. Amen.

5

A Sheep of God's Flock

Psalm 23

The LORD is my shepherd; I shall not want . . . Surely goodness and mercy shall follow me all the days of my life, and I shall dwell in the house of the LORD forever.

(Ps 23:1, 6)

PSALM 23 IS THE best known and most deeply loved of all the psalms. I love it, and I imagine you do too, because it is so personal. It isn't just "our" psalm; it is "my" psalm. "The Lord is *my* Shepherd . . . He leads *me* beside still waters . . . He prepares *me* a table in the presence of *my* enemies . . . His goodness and mercy will follow *me* all the days of *my* life" (there are no fewer than seventeen first-person singular pronouns in just six verses!).

God has given us this beautiful song because he wants to hear each of us say with confidence and relief, "The Lord knows and cares about me—my friendships, my needs, my joys, my hardships, and my hopes." Take a moment to read Ps 23 aloud now:

The LORD is my shepherd; I shall not want.
    He makes me lie down in green pastures.
He leads me beside still waters.
    He restores my soul.

He leads me in paths of righteousness
for his name's sake.

Even though I walk through the valley of the shadow of death,
I will fear no evil,
for you are with me;
your rod and your staff,
they comfort me.

You prepare a table before me
in the presence of my enemies;
you anoint my head with oil;
my cup overflows.
Surely goodness and mercy shall follow me
all the days of my life,
and I shall dwell in the house of the LORD
forever. (Ps 23:1–6)

It's not always easy for us to believe these words are true. Assuming they were known to David because he had composed them in his youth, we can still imagine him stumbling over them as Saul was chasing him through the wilderness trying to kill him. Jesus probably struggled to believe them as his enemies beat him and spat on him. But here they are, designed for our encouragement, telling us that God is our shepherd and friend, in good times and in bad.

JESUS THE SHEEP

There is a dimension to Ps 23 that you may not have noticed. It will jump off the page if you imagine Jesus saying it to himself as a boy and later as a man. You and I are apt to think of Jesus as the Shepherd of the psalm—and for good reason, since he invites us to call him that.[1] But he was also a sheep once.

Listen to Caroline Marie Noel's hymn, "At the Name of Jesus Every Knee Shall Bow." It vividly describes the choice God made to become a sheep. Here is one of the stanzas:

Humbled for a season to receive a name
From the lips of sinners unto whom he came,
Faithfully he bore it spotless to the last,

1. See John 10:14.

> Brought it back victorious, when from death he past.[2]

God's Son became Jesus of Nazareth, named by his parents like newborns generally are. He received a name because he wanted to learn what he wants you and me to learn—to trust God in good times and bad. Reading Ps 23 as Jesus' song opens our eyes to that experience.

A PORTRAIT OF JESUS

Verse 1

> The LORD is my shepherd, I shall not want. (Ps 23:1)

Starving in the wilderness, tempted to prove his identity by turning stones into bread, Jesus trusts God to provide when and how God will provide. He waits on God for bread, as we all must. A particularly lovely expression of Jesus' confidence in God's provision occurs one afternoon in Samaria, when Jesus forgoes his midday meal to spend time with a lonely Samaritan women, later explaining himself with these remarkable words: "My food is to do the will of him who sent me."[3]

Verse 2–3a

> He makes me lie down in green pastures.
> He leads me beside still waters.
> He restores my soul. (Ps 23:2–3a)

Surrounded by enormous and relentless human need, people clamoring for bread and healing, hounding him from one Galilean town to another, Jesus routinely chooses and finds rest in his heavenly Shepherd's company. One such moment appears after the feeding of the 5000:

> Immediately he made his disciples get into the boat and go before him to the other side, to Bethsaida, while he dismissed the crowd. And after he had taken leave of them, he went up on the mountain to pray. (Mark 6:45–46)

2. Noel, "At the Name," 163–64.
3. John 4:34.

Verse 3b

> He leads me in the paths of righteousness
> for his name's sake. (Ps 23:3b)

God's leading goes back to Jesus' infancy, when his parents bring him to the temple to be consecrated. It continues through his childhood as he returns yearly on Passover, so whetting his appetite for God's paths that when Jesus comes to Jerusalem for the festival at age twelve, he stays behind for days, "sitting among the teachers, listening to them and asking them questions" (Luke 2:46). By the time of his wilderness testing, God's ways have found such firm rooting in Jesus that Satan can't touch him, no matter how extreme his circumstances. Living "by every word that comes from the mouth of God" (Matt 4:4), Jesus answers every assault with Scripture, even the one that misuses Scripture to lead him astray.[4]

Verse 5

> You prepare a table before me
> in the presence of my enemies;
> you anoint my head with oil;
> my cup overflows. (Ps 23:5)

Jesus makes many enemies, but their power and hatred never faze him. His life overflows with love and majesty. Even at the bitter end, as his enemies prevail over him, he endures them with quiet dignity at his arrest and trial and even prays for them.[5]

Verse 4

> Even though I walk through the valley of the shadow of death,
> I will fear no evil,
> for you are with me;
> your rod and your staff,
> they comfort me. (Ps 23:4)

4. See Matt 4:1–11 and parallels.
5. See John 8:31–59, John 18:1–11, Matt 26:57–68, and Luke 23:34.

Alone in the garden of Gethsemane while his disciples sleep, and overwhelmed at the prospect of his crucifixion, Jesus fights his way back to trusting submission and finds refreshment from God's hand:

> "Father, if you are willing, remove this cup from me. Nevertheless, not my will, but yours, be done." And there appeared to him an angel from heaven, strengthening him. (Luke 22:42–43)

Notice that verse 4 says, "I will *fear* no evil," not "I will *experience* no evil." Jesus' struggle to trust God takes place, as does ours, in the face of evil. I vividly remember clinging to these words in the middle of the night before I was to speak to Christians in a heavily Muslim district of Bangladesh. Their church had lost its roof, along with a number of its members, during anti-Christian rioting just months before, and there was no knowing what might happen to me. With Christ's help I had to fight my way to trusting submission.

COLLAPSE

But why should I have trusted God that night in Bangladesh—why should I have believed the promises of Ps 23 when the psalm failed Jesus at the end of his life? Think of verses 4 and 6:

> For you are with me;
>   your rod and your staff,
>   they comfort me . . .
> Surely goodness and mercy shall follow me
>   all the days of my life. (Ps 23:4, 6)

In the garden of Gethsemane, there were the comforting angels, and, with them, the comfort of God himself. That comfort "followed" (v 6) Jesus through the crisis and enabled him to stand up to his enemies during his trial and to bear the terrible scourging that followed.

But the dreadful anguish in the garden comes back, without relief, as Jesus dies. God is *not* "with him; [his] rod and staff [*do not*] comfort" him. If ever a sheep needed, and deserved, the heavenly Shepherd's "goodness and mercy" (v 6), it was Jesus on Good Friday. But on that scandalous day, no mercy came. The comfort of Ps 23 collapsed in ruins. The Shepherd deserted his sheep. The perfect sheep became the dying lamb:

> He was oppressed, and he was afflicted . . .
> like a lamb that is led to the slaughter. (Isa 53:7)

ASTONISHING TRUST—FOR OUR SAKES

With the scandal comes a great faithfulness. For Jesus the sheep still hangs on through a degree of ruin and misery we cannot measure. He trusts his Shepherd still, crying from the cross, "*My* God, *my* God, why have you forsaken me?" (Matt 27:46). Forsaken by his Father, utterly alone in outer darkness, Jesus still trusts, calling God his own. At this moment Jesus expresses the deep trust of Ps 23 in a way we never could and will never need to. We will never have to cry from hell as Jesus did.

There may be times when it seems that the Shepherd has abandoned you. But this will never be so if you belong to Jesus. For the "collapse" of Ps 23 in Jesus' case happened because he chose to be "the Lamb of God, who takes away the sin of the world" (John 1:29),[6] including yours. Your sins are gone. They will never again have the power to banish you. Even at your darkest moments you can with confidence say, "For you are with me; your rod and your staff, they comfort me," because on Good Friday, Jesus could not. As you lay dying, you can gasp, "I will dwell in the house of the Lord forever," because on Good Friday, Jesus chose to be thrown out of God's house.

Lord Jesus, heavenly Shepherd, you were a sheep once. You spent a lifetime doing what you ask me to do—trusting God to feed, direct, comfort, and care for you. You had to lean on your Father, just as I do, in good times and bad, among friends and before enemies. And then, at the end, you did what I will never have to do: you trusted your Father as hell closed in over you, as wrath over my sins bore down upon you, as you carried my sins away into darkness.

I wonder at your devotion to the Father and your love for me. I confess with shame that I don't trust you as you deserve. I too easily give way to fear and grumbling. I grow impatient and bitter in trial. I often want comfort more than I want you. Forgive my doubts. Forgive my cold heart. Amen.

6. Jesus made this breathtakingly vivid when, at the Last Supper, he gave the disciples himself (rather than lamb) to eat: "Take, eat; this is my body" (Matt 26:26). Revelation celebrates his self-giving repeatedly, calling Jesus "the Lamb" nearly thirty times. I am indebted to Kathy Keller for this reminder.

6

Delighting

Psalm 34

I will bless the LORD at all times. His praise shall continually be in my mouth.

(Ps 34:1)

THE PSALMS ARE FULL of delight. Here is a sampling:

> Oh, magnify the LORD with me
> and let us exalt his name together! (Ps 34:3)

> One thing have I asked of the LORD,
> that will I seek after:
> that I may dwell in the house of the LORD
> all the days of my life,
> to gaze upon the beauty of the LORD
> and to inquire in his temple. (Ps 27:4)

> Not to us, O LORD, not to us, but to
> your name, give glory. (Ps 115:1)

> I was glad when they said to me,
> "Let us go to the house of the LORD!" (Ps 122:1)

> In the way of your testimonies I delight

> as much as in all riches.
> I will meditate on your precepts
> and fix my eyes on your ways.
> I will delight in your statutes;
> I will not forget your word . . .
> My soul is consumed with longing
> for your rules at all times. (Ps 119:14–16, 20)

We instinctively read these words as our own songs of devotion. And as we do, they have a certain resonance if we are believers. That new person inside us, upon whose heart the Spirit is writing the law of God, rises up in us and cries, "Yes! This is who I am! This is what I want!" Such expressions of delight describe us, motivate us, and inspire us.

OUR SONGS, REALLY?

But if you and I are honest, there is another part of us that finds these songs troubling. Are we really, and always, as single-mindedly God-centered as we claim in Ps 27:4? Are we really, and always, "delight[ing]" (Ps 119:16) in what God has to say? You might be on Sunday morning, perhaps, during a particularly stirring song or after a particularly stirring message. But how about on Wednesday at work, when someone else gets credit for something you did? How about late Saturday night, when you are alone, tired, and depressed, and your mind is drawn toward internet pornography? How about Friday when you are obsessing about mastering a soccer move or a difficult passage on the violin—bitter and anxious because it isn't coming together?

- Think of Ps 122:

  > I was glad when they said to me,
  > "Let us go to the house of the LORD!" (Ps 122:1)

  Are you always really glad to go to church, especially when it means you have to interact with certain people who are weird, or pushy, or rude, or sing flat? Aren't you often distracted, tired, and half-hearted?

- Think of Ps 115:

  > Not to us, O LORD, not to us, but to
  > your name, give glory. (Ps 115:1)

> Does God's glory always take a higher place than your own? How about when a better preacher moves to town and eclipses your ministry—or when a new kid shows up for the audition who is better than you are and gets the part—or when another researcher beats you to press with the results you have been working on for years?

The delights and aspirations in verses like these sometimes depress us. And if they never depress us, then we have another problem. We have managed to lie to ourselves. Like modern day Pharisees, we have convinced ourselves that we meet the standard, that we are better than the people who do not know as much Bible as we do, or who don't worship as enthusiastically as we do, or are not as nice at church as we are, or do not appear as sold out to God as we do.

GETTING PAST THE TENSION BETWEEN ASPIRATION AND REALITY

How do we get past the sometimes-depressing tension I am describing—the tension between what ought to characterize our devotion and what actually characterizes it? We do it by listening for another voice, in addition to our own, in these words. We listen for the voice of our brother Jesus, for whom these expressions of delight were always genuine.

If you do this, a number of things happen. First, you will begin to see Jesus more vividly. When Jesus made his way to Jerusalem amidst the praises of his disciples, refusing to silence the worshiping disciples, when Jesus sang psalms with his disciples on the night of his betrayal, and when he told them at the Last Supper, "I have earnestly desired to eat this Passover with you before I suffer" (Luke 22:15),[1] he was living out his delight in the company and worship of the church. He really was "glad when they said to [him], Let us go into the house of the Lord."

Think again of Ps 115: "Not to us, O LORD, not to us, but to your name, give glory" (Ps 115:1). When Jesus thanked God at the feeding of the multitude, when he refused to let them make him king afterward,[2] and when, on his last night, he prayed, "Father . . . glorify your Son that the Son may glorify you" (John 17:1), he was living these words far more fully than you and I are yet able to.

1. See Luke 19:35–40 and Mark 14:26.
2. See John 6:11, 15.

Learning to hear Jesus' voice in all these expressions of devotion will likely encourage you. It will remind you that you have a fellow traveler, an elder brother, who loves God genuinely, despite all the distractions and impediments he faced. It will remind you that Jesus joined us here not to condemn us for our tepid devotion but to help us love God better.

When you see the gap between the psalms' fervent love for God and your half-hearted love, don't deny it. Let the psalms bother you. But do something else. Ask Jesus for help.

JESUS, OUR COVERING

But don't just ask for Jesus' help. Thank him that you already have it (this gets at a second thing that can happen when we meet Jesus in the psalms of delight). Paul tells us that God has made Jesus "⌊our⌋ righteousness" (1 Cor 1:30), which means that we already look beautiful to the Father. Somehow, if we belong to Jesus, his joy in his Father's company hides beneath itself our often cold and divided hearts, making our faith and service, however flawed, a delight to the Father's heart. Isaiah experienced this and it encouraged him deeply:

> I will greatly rejoice in the LORD;
> my soul shall exult in my God,
> for he has clothed me with the garments of salvation;
> he has covered me with the robe of righteousness,
> as a bridegroom decks himself like a priest with a beautiful headdress,
> and as a bride adorns herself with her jewels. (Isa 61:10)

God has "dressed you up" so thoroughly in Jesus (theologians call this union with Christ) that when he looks upon you, he sees his Son and for that reason delights in you as fervently as he delights in him, despite everything in you that still needs fixing.

NEW SONG RISING

Think about your union with Christ for any length of time, and it will give your love for God a genuine boost, just like being genuinely welcomed onto a team encourages you to play your best. Look again at Ps 27 to see how this transforming dynamic works:

> One thing have I asked of the LORD,
> that will I seek after:
> that I may dwell in the house of the LORD
> all the days of my life,
> to gaze upon the beauty of the LORD
> and to inquire in his temple. (Ps 27:4)

When we hear these words solely as "our song"—as an example of the sort of attitude we are supposed to have—the psalm will not in the long run help us very much. It will, in fact, tend to discourage us because we don't measure up to it. But if we also hear these inspiring words as Jesus' song, sung on our behalf through all the days of his dedicated life, and know it to be a song that God hears and accepts as if it were our own, then the song will mysteriously gain strength in us. We will find ourselves genuinely loving God more because we are learning that, thanks to Jesus, everything is fundamentally and forever OK between God and us. He is not waiting for us to get the melody right before he can enjoy our singing. Another, better song has gone out before ours and covers ours.

Notice something else, equally encouraging. The new, genuine, grace-based song that is starting to rise in you is never going to die. Right now, its faulty notes are covered by the song of Jesus. But at its center it is a good song, and it will last, because it is the song of Christ's Spirit in you. It will not become fully yours until the end, but it has begun already.

WORSHIP LEADER

I suspect that hearing Jesus' voice in the songs of delight, especially if you note that so many of them are "we songs" (think back to our discussion in chapter three), will encourage you in yet one more way. Listen again to Ps 34:

> Oh, magnify the LORD with me,
> and let *us* exalt his name together! (Ps 34:3)

The "us" in these words includes Jesus. It features him, in fact. Whenever we gather for worship, Jesus joins in. In fact, he summons us: "Dear friends," he cries out, "brothers and sisters, let's exalt the Lord together."

You may find it hard to get your mind around this, for, of course, we are worshiping Jesus when we sing God's praises. But there is always more going on. We are also singing *with* him (not just *to* him)—and this is true even when we sing flat or half-heartedly or mindlessly. He is always there, like one of the professional "ringers" my choral director brings in just before our concerts to bring our singing up toward par. Sunday mornings may need some improvement—more attentiveness, more fervency. But God still loves it when we gather to praise him. For Jesus is there.

I have only noted a tiny sampling of the songs of joy. You will find them all over the Psalter. Let them be your songs. Let them wash over you. Let them challenge your priorities and appetites. But don't stop there. Let them take you into the heart of Jesus, the one true worshiper (we call him the Second Adam), who lives in and among us to make us beautiful.

Heavenly Father, I wonder at your joy over me. My flawed efforts at obedience, my distracted songs of worship, delight you even in their hypocrisy, not because you delight in hypocrisy, but because you delight in your Son, who brings me with him into your presence.

Thank you for your gift to me in my elder brother. Thank you for Jesus' single-minded devotion, for his deep and continuous worship—all of which he has laid over me like a wedding garment, so that I look and sound like him to you, despite my flaws. I bless you for his Spirit who lives in me, who gets hold of me increasingly as I seek to follow, and who guarantees that my love for you will one day be like his, full and pure beyond measure.

Rise up in me, Lord Jesus. Make my love for the Father more like yours today. Make my worship more like yours today. Send your Spirit to write your songs on my heart. Amen.

7

Trusting

Psalm 139

Search me, O God, and know my heart! Try me and know my thoughts! And see if there be any grievous way in me, and lead me in the way everlasting!

(Ps 139:23–24)

Psalm 139 is one of my favorites. An intimate meditation on God's love, it develops in three stanzas, erupts in angry vexation, and ends in a prayer that draws its language from the opening verse. Here it is, broken out:

Stanza 1: You know me.

> O LORD, you have searched me and known me!
> You know when I sit down and when I rise up;
> you discern my thoughts from afar.
> You search out my path and my lying down
> and are acquainted with all my ways.
> Even before a word is on my tongue,
> behold, O LORD, you know it altogether.
> You hem me in, behind and before,
> and lay your hand upon me.
> Such knowledge is too wonderful for me;
> it is high; I cannot attain it. (Ps 139:1–6)

Stanza 2: You are always with me.

Where shall I go from your Spirit?
    Or where shall I flee from your presence?
If I ascend to heaven, you are there!
    If I make my bed in Sheol, you are there!
If I take the wings of the morning
    and dwell in the uttermost parts of the sea,
even there your hand shall lead me,
    and your right hand shall hold me.
If I say, "Surely the darkness shall cover me,
    and the light about me be night,"
even the darkness is not dark to you;
    the night is bright as the day,
    for darkness is as light with you. (Ps 139:7–12)

Stanza 3: You made me and think about me all the time.

For you formed my inward parts;
    you knitted me together in my mother's womb.
I praise you, for I am fearfully and wonderfully made.
Wonderful are your works;
    my soul knows it very well.
My frame was not hidden from you,
when I was being made in secret,
    intricately woven in the depths of the earth.
Your eyes saw my unformed substance;
in your book were written, every one of them,
    the days that were formed for me,
    when as yet there were none of them.

How precious to me are your thoughts, O God!
    How vast is the sum of them!
If I would count them, they are more than the sand.
    I awake, and I am still with you. (Ps 139:13–18)

Cry of vexation: I am furious at anyone who speaks ill of you!

Oh that you would slay the wicked, O God!
    O men of blood, depart from me!
They speak against you with malicious intent;
    your enemies take your name in vain!
Do I not hate those who hate you, O LORD?
    And do I not loathe those who rise up against you?
I hate them with complete hatred;

I count them my enemies. (Ps 139:19–22)

Prayer: Borrowing language from the opening.

Search me, O God, and know my heart!
Try me and know my thoughts!
And see if there be any grievous way in me,
and lead me in the way everlasting! (Ps 139:23–24)

FINDING SERENITY

Before we listen for Jesus' voice in this song, let's take time to listen for ours. Notice first how intimate the language is. This psalm isn't about "us"; it's about "me." Like Ps 23 it brims over with "I," "me," and "my" (forty-eight of them in just twenty-four verses). If we can say this psalm and mean it, we will find deep serenity no matter what life throws at us. Regardless of what people (bosses, parents, friends, enemies, or philosophers) may say to or about us, regardless of what circumstances may suggest, regardless of how good or successful we have managed to be, we will find rest and delight knowing that we are precious to the one Person whose evaluation of us matters the most:

I praise you because I am fearfully and wonderfully made . . .
How precious to me are your thoughts [about me!], O God!
How vast is the sum of them!
If I could count them, they are more than the sand. (Ps 139:14, 17–18)

Even if no one knows or recognizes us, God does. He takes note of us with the sort of knowledge that misses nothing ("You have searched me and known me;" "you discern my thoughts from afar"), is inescapable ("If I ascend to heaven, you are there! If I make my bed in Sheol, you are there!"), watches over us ("in your book were written, every one of them, the days that were formed for me"), and does not let us get away with anything ("You hem me in, behind and before, and lay your hand on me").

God is like the internet of our nightmares, only worse. He not only has the record of all our searches—he also knows they are ours, he knows where we live, and he is after us. This would be terrifying if he did not love us so much. But the whole point of Ps 139 is that he does.

JUSTIFIABLE FURY: DEEP SUBMISSION

I suspect that the outburst after the third stanza jars you like a crash of symbols in the midst of a lullaby. My beloved grandmother was so disturbed by verses 19–22 that she drew a big red "x" through them in her Bible. What are we to do with them?

A story may help. Once, when my dad was in his eighties and still driving, he was side-swiped by an impatient young motorist, who made an obscene gesture and remark as he roared past him. My father was a kind and generous man—a veteran who had risked his life in WWII—a man who had loved my mother and his four children faithfully for many years. When Dad told me this story, relating it with a patient, self-deprecating laugh, I wanted to find that young motorist and strangle him.

My reaction was a little bit like David's in verses 19–22, and it arose from the same place. How could anyone treat with disrespect a person I knew to be so good?!

Swept up in the goodness and care of God, David ends the psalm by laying his life at God's feet: "Search me . . . Know my heart . . . See if there be any grievous way in me . . . Lead me."

WHY SHOULD WE BELIEVE ALL THIS?

Such is the comforting account we find of ourselves in Ps 139. But why should we believe it? Why should we believe in a love that will not let us go, that searches us so thoroughly, that thinks about us all the time, and that follows us everywhere, even into the darkness of death?

Let me push the question even harder. Biologist Richard Dawkins writes:

> The total amount of suffering in the natural world is beyond all decent contemplation . . . The universe that we observe has precisely the properties we should expect if there is, at bottom, no designer, no purpose, no evil, no good, nothing but pitiless indifference.[1]

According to Dawkins our dreams of human significance, of cosmic welcome—of goodness and love aimed toward us—are delusional. How can we be sure Dawkins isn't right? How can we be sure that David wasn't indulging in religious wishful thinking when he wrote Ps 139?

1. Dawkins, *Eden*, 131–32, 133.

JESUS' STORY—NOT JUST OURS

Here is how we can be confident in the assurances of Ps 139. The God whose love we celebrate with David demonstrated that love when he made the experience of the psalm his own, from our side, as a fellow traveler. Since the appearance of Jesus, Ps 139 has described not only our experience but God's.

Try a little experiment. Go back to the beginning of the chapter and read Ps 139 through aloud. But before you do imagine that you are Jesus at age twelve, shortly after your anxious parents have found you in the temple, rebuked you for getting lost, and ordered you home with them (you will find the story in Luke 2:41–51). Imagine yourself, as Jesus, quietly praying, "You lay your hand on me" as you submit to your parents and head home.

Now read the psalm again, this time imagining you are Jesus praying it in the midst of your anguish in the garden of Gethsemane. Hear him praying, "Lead me in the way everlasting!" as he faces the cross.

God the Son was "knitted . . . together in [his] mother's womb" (like you were). God the Son received from his Father (as have you), "a book, where were written, every one of them, the days that were formed for [him]." God the Son submitted (as you and I must) to the Father's "hem[ming] . . . in"—to constraints of circumstance and obligation like yours, and in excess of yours: to a body, to poverty, to homelessness, to unpredictable friends, to despotic rulers, and to suffering.

In the end, God the Son chose to be hemmed in by something that need never ensnare us. When we read in verse 12, "even the darkness is not dark to you," we mean that God "sees" us in our darkest times and will "see us through" them. But when Jesus endured the darkness on Good Friday, he was alone, cast into what he had earlier called the "outer darkness,"[2] forsaken by God as he bore our sin and its punishment as our substitute.

PROFOUND AND WELL-INFORMED LOVE

What drove God to embrace Ps 139 from the inside, to own it as your human brother? What drove him to endure the loss of its comforting assurances? It was his well-informed love—a love that knows what we need most deeply and will not rest until we get what we need. Because God searches our hearts, because he knows our rising, our sitting, and our lying down,

2. See Matt 8:12.

because he knows our thoughts, words, and motives, because nothing whatsoever escapes his notice, God knows that the trusting and joyful submission in Ps 139 describes us only on our best days—and even then only imperfectly.

God knows that we do not always want to be truly known, that we often bridle at his loving constraints and wise protection, and that we even seek at times to flee from him, preferring to live the fantasy that we are our own makers and owners. He knows that our half-hearted devotion can never earn us a place by his side. God knows that we need to be rescued from our self-destructive selves.

And so, God made Ps 139 his own, living out its trusting delight in your place, as your brother. And he did so not just occasionally but all his days. He did this so that on his final day, the day that God had "ordained for [him]," he could offer his life in exchange for yours, taking your haphazard faithfulness as if it were his own and covering you with his own moral and spiritual beauty.

HOPE FOR THE FINAL MORNING

Notice the end of verse 18:

> I awake, and I am still with you. (Ps 139:18)

David drew great delight and consolation from knowing that after the uncertainty, danger, and oblivion of each night, he would awake yet again to a God who was there, to a God who had never left him. You perhaps share that consolation. But what about the "morning" after the great "sleep" at the end of your life? And what about the Great Morning at the end of human history when God will summon you for judgment? Will you be *with him* then—known, loved, and welcomed, despite all that he knows about you? The answer is yes. It will be yes because Ps 139 was your Messiah's song too.

Searching Redeemer, your love will never give up on me. You know everything about me. You pursue me everywhere. You made me and order my days to my final breath. You order all things for my good.

I know you love me this way, not because I always seek you but because you came in search of me. You sought me by joining me here as a fellow creature and by living out the sort of life I ought to live but do not.

Whereas I am often ungrateful for the way God made me, Lord Jesus, you readily chose your mother's womb. Whereas I often prefer to be left to myself, you always sought your Father's presence. Whereas I do not always welcome the Father's leading, Lord Jesus, you did, even when it brought you to the cross.

Thank you for loving me with such determination. Forgive my independent and ungrateful spirit. Send your Spirit to make me angry at my mistrust. Make me more like you. Amen.

8

Desolation

Psalm 88

I, O LORD, cry to you; in the morning my prayer comes before you. O LORD, why do you cast my soul away? Why do you hide your face from me?

(Ps 88:13–14)

PSALM 88 IS ABOUT as dark as any psalm gets—and without relief. Most every other dark psalm has an upturn at some point but not this one. Take some time to read Ps 88 aloud now. As you do, imagine Jesus processing it at some point during his time among us.

O LORD, God of my salvation;
    I cry out day and night before you.
Let my prayer come before you;
    incline your ear to my cry!

For my soul is full of troubles,
    and my life draws near to Sheol.
I am counted among those who go down to the pit;
    I am a man who has no strength,
like one set loose among the dead,
    like the slain that lie in the grave,
like those whom you remember no more,

for they are cut off from your hand.
You have put me in the depths of the pit,
in the regions dark and deep.
Your wrath lies heavy upon me,
and you overwhelm me with all your waves.

You have caused my companions to shun me;
you have made me a horror to them.
I am shut in so that I cannot escape;
my eye grows dim through sorrow.
Every day I call upon you, O LORD;
I spread out my hands to you.
Do you work wonders for the dead?
Do the departed rise up to praise you?

Is your steadfast love declared in the grave,
or your faithfulness in Abaddon?
Are your wonders known in the darkness,
or your righteousness in the land of forgetfulness?

But I, O LORD, cry to you;
in the morning my prayer comes before you.
O LORD, why do you cast my soul away?
Why do you hide your face from me?
Afflicted and close to death from my youth up,
I suffer your terrors; I am helpless.
Your wrath has swept over me;
your dreadful assaults destroy me.
They surround me like a flood all day long;
they close in on me together.
You have caused my beloved and my friend to shun me;
my companions have become darkness. (Ps 88:1–18)

UNRELENTING MISERY

You and I might read these words and wonder how they found their way into the Bible (can you imagine saying them in church, even if you felt them to be true?). The psalmist cries out to God repeatedly—"day and night" (Ps 88:1) and "every day" (Ps 88:9)—and receives no response. His inner life is a shambles ("my soul is full of troubles" [Ps 88:3]) and his reputation is in ruins ("You have made me a horror" to "my companions" [Ps 88:8]).

His mind is wracked with confusion and frustration: "Is your steadfast love declared in the grave?" (Ps 88:11). I love you and am faithful to you—so why are you shutting me down? I don't get it!

He is profoundly lonely. His friends "shun [him]" (Ps 88:8): not even his dearest companion ("my beloved" [Ps 88:18]), the one person he could always rely on, will have anything to do with him. And God is nowhere to be found, except perhaps as his judge, drowning him in condemnation ("You overwhelm me with all your waves" [Ps 88:7]).

And the miseries won't stop. Day and night they continue so that he is worn out and almost blind from them ("My eye grows dim through sorrow" [Ps 88:9]).

We might read this account and find ourselves saying, "Thank God that things are not like this for me!" Or, we might, in a bad moment, snap at someone who talks this way: "Oh, get over it! It's not that bad!" Or, we might think of someone we love for whom these words (or some of them) are true. In this case, our hearts would be troubled. We would likely feel something of their fear, isolation, forsakenness, and helplessness. We would likely pray and look for ways to help.

MEETING JESUS

We can easily imagine Jesus responding in the last of these ways. He was a "man of sorrows" (Isa 53:3), in large part because our griefs and difficulties weighed on him all the time.[1] He was "deeply moved in his spirit and greatly troubled"[2] when he beheld the grief of Mary, Martha, and their friends at the graveside of Lazarus. Beholding a widow grieving over her dead son, "he had compassion on her and said to her, 'Do not weep'" (Luke 7:13).

Jesus was a good man, and human misery got to him the way our children's miseries get to us. But there was an added dimension to Jesus' grief, for he was more than a good man. He was the perfect man, the true "image of . . . God" (Col 1:15). He knew in his own experience what human life was supposed to be like—its closeness to God, its harmony with others,

1. This is not to say, of course that gloom enveloped him. He "rejoice[s] in the Holy Spirit" when his Father shows his power to the disciples (see Luke 10:21–22). He celebrates with his friends, turning water into wine to enhance a wedding party (see John 2:1–11). He welcomes his disciples' lack of fasting because "the bridegroom is with them" (Matt 9:15).

2. John 11:33. The Greek for "greatly troubled" means "furious."

and the peace of a clear conscience. He saw and felt, as no one else could, the enormous gap between what is and what ought to be in human experience, and this broke his heart because he loved people.

WHAT IS AND WHAT OUGHT TO BE

In *Perelandra*, C. S. Lewis tells the story of Edwin Ransom, a philologist who finds himself on the unfallen but threatened planet of Venus. He encounters Weston, a fellow earthling who has lost his humanity in the service of a great evil. He finds him mauling the legs of scores of frog-like creatures and leaving them slowly to die:

> The hind legs [of the first one Ransom encountered] had been almost torn off . . .They were so damaged that the frog could not leap. On earth it would have been merely a nasty sight, but up to this moment Ransom had as yet seen nothing dead or spoiled in Perelandra, and it was like a blow in the face . . . It was like the first lie from the mouth of a friend on whose truth one was willing to stake a thousand pounds.[3]

What happens when a good person comes upon a great evil? The person shakes with horror, as Ransom does. He cries out, "This cannot go on! Something must be done!" As the story continues, Ransom comes to the conviction that he must fight Weston to the death.

WHAT MUST I DO, FATHER?

Think again about Jesus. What happens when the Son of God, the one true man, comes upon the sort of human misery that Ps 88 makes so vivid? What happens when he notes that this misery is not an isolated case but is in some measure the experience and destiny of people throughout the world, people he loves? He cries, "Father, this cannot continue! What can be done, what must I do, to end it?"

We do not know precisely how or when the answer to this question dawned on Jesus. But by the time he decided to make his way to Jerusalem to die, he plainly knew it. The Father and his own heart had told him that he must erase this suffering from the earth, and that he must do so by enduring it himself: he must himself be "put . . . in the depths of the pit" (Ps 88:6);

3. Lewis, *Perelandra*, 108–9.

he must be trapped hopelessly in misery (be "shut in so that [he] cannot escape" [Ps 88:8]); he must be utterly without human comfort, a "horror" (Ps 88:8) to his friends. There must be, as in the case of Ps 88, no let-up in the misery. And, in the end, the misery must extend to abandonment by God himself. The God known to him as "my salvation" (Ps 88:1), the God of "steadfast love" (Ps 88:11), must cut him off.

JESUS' DESOLATION FOR OURS

We will never fully understand the answer to Jesus' heartbroken cry as he died, echoed in verse 14: "Why do you hide your face from me?" But the Bible and Jesus himself teach repeatedly that it was necessary.[4] God's Son had to be our substitute in the fullness of our sufferings so that he might win back and preserve our joy by his own sorrows. Perhaps Isa 53 came to Jesus' mind as he processed Ps 88:

> He was despised and rejected by men,
> a man of sorrows and acquainted with grief;
> and as one from whom men hide their faces
> he was despised and we esteemed him not.
> Surely he has borne our griefs
> and carried our sorrows;
> yet we esteemed him stricken,
> smitten by God, and afflicted.
> But he was pierced for our transgressions;
> he was crushed for our iniquities;
> upon him was the chastisement that brought us peace,
> and with his wounds we are healed. (Isa 53:3–5)

BRINGING OUR SORROWS TO JESUS

Jesus never promises immediate delivery from the things that devastate us. I have had to sit for what seemed interminable seasons with shattering circumstances, and you may have also. But Jesus does promise to walk through devastation with us. And he invites us to shout at him from the deep places, or simply groan in his direction, if we are out of words. He knows our sorrows from inside them, and we can be confident of this because Ps 88 was his song.

4. See Matt 16:21, Luke 24:25–26, and elsewhere.

Lord Jesus, I don't know why heartbreak, loneliness, and pain can at times be so overwhelming and relentless. But I know that I can come to you with my troubles, even when I am out of words and can barely speak, even when I am furious with frustration and waiting. I know that you will never push me away, even when it feels like that is what you are doing. I know this because you have suffered every desolation yourself. And you have suffered even more than I. For whereas it appears at times that God has abandoned me—even though he hasn't—you were in reality abandoned by the Father when you carried my sins into the darkness.

You were under no moral obligation to join me in this broken place. You came to me simply because you wanted to. And somehow, in the mysterious interchange that I will never fully understand, joining me in my brokenness has broken its grip upon me. Your stripes have begun to heal me, and your chosen grief will rescue me from every grief.

Dear Father, you suffered as well. I can never measure what it cost you to turn from your Son when he needed you the most. I can never measure how deeply Jesus' heartbreak broke your own heart. But I know that it did, and that you endured that grief because you shared his love for me. Thank you. I love you back. I trust you. Amen.

9

Determination

Psalm 132

I will not enter my house or get into my bed, I will not give sleep to my eyes or slumber to my eyelids, until I find a place for the LORD, a dwelling place for the Mighty One of Jacob.

(Ps 132:3–5)

READ PS 132 ALOUD, and as you do imagine Jesus allowing its words to shape his calling and the urgency of it:

Remember, O LORD, in David's favor,
all the hardships he endured,
how he swore to the LORD
and vowed to the Mighty One of Jacob,
"I will not enter my house
or get into my bed,
I will not give sleep to my eyes
or slumber to my eyelids,
until I find a place for the LORD,
a dwelling place for the Mighty One of Jacob."

Behold, we heard of it in Ephrathah;
we found it in the fields of Jaar.

"Let us go to his dwelling place;
 let us worship at his footstool!"

Arise, O LORD, and go to your resting place,
 you and the ark of your might.
Let your priests be clothed with righteousness,
 and let your saints shout for joy.
For the sake of your servant David,
 do not turn away the face of your anointed one.

The LORD swore to David a sure oath
 from which he will not turn back:
"One of the sons of your body
 I will set on your throne.
If your sons keep my covenant
 and my testimonies that I shall teach them,
their sons also forever
 shall sit on your throne."
For the LORD has chosen Zion;
 he has desired it for his dwelling place:
"This is my resting place forever;
 here I will dwell, for I have desired it.
I will abundantly bless her provisions;
 I will satisfy her poor with bread.
Her priests I will clothe with salvation,
 and her saints will shout for joy.
There I will make a horn to sprout for David;
 I have prepared a lamp for my anointed.
His enemies I will clothe with shame,
 but on him his crown will shine." (Ps 132:1–18)

BRINGING GOD HOME

The background to this psalm (Jesus would have known it) is the story of the ark of the covenant, the gold-covered box that represented God's throne and presence. As David had risen to power, the ark was homeless and had always been so. It had wandered for forty years in the wilderness with Israel.[1] It had languished in Shiloh, twenty-five miles north of Jerusalem,

1. Exodus 40:34–38 describes the movement of the tabernacle through the wilderness years: the ark moved with it. Josh 3–4 describes the movement of the ark and the people over the Jordan and into the land of promise.

after the conquest of the land. It had been captured by the Philistines and paraded through the Philistines' temples and cities until it had caused so much damage that they had put it on an oxcart and sent it away. Once back within Israel's borders, the ark had languished for another twenty years in a place called Kiriath-jearim, an out-of-the-way town in the hills, eight miles west of Jerusalem.[2]

But David changed all this. Once he had subdued the Philistines and captured Jerusalem, he had fetched the ark with an enormous entourage and brought it home to Jerusalem with great joy:

> So David went and brought up the ark of God . . . with rejoicing. And when those who bore the ark of the LORD had gone six steps, he sacrificed an ox and a fattened animal. And David danced before the LORD with all his might . . . So David and all the house of Israel brought up the ark of the LORD with shouting and with the sound of the horn. (2 Sam 6:12–15)

David had given himself so earnestly to this task, he had refused to "give sleep to [his] eyes" (Ps 132:4) until it was accomplished, not because he wanted the gold-covered box in Jerusalem but because he wanted God there: "Arise, *O LORD*, and go to your resting place" (Ps 132:8) was the cry of his heart. And that resting place was Jerusalem ("Zion" [Ps 132:13] and her people: David and "the sons of [his] body" (Ps 132:11), "her poor" (Ps 132:15), "her priests . . . and her saints" (Ps 132:16).

JESUS' DETERMINATION

Imagine Jesus processing this psalm. At some point during his earthly life he would have come to the conviction that he was the "son of [David's] body" whom God had promised to "set on [his] throne" (Ps 132:11), and that that enthronement would be "forever" (Ps 132:12). For this reason, he would have embraced David's mission and zeal as his own. Imagine how Jesus might have reworked the words of the psalm in the light of his own calling:

> I will not rest, Father, until I have brought you home to my people. I will be homeless, wandering the countryside with "nowhere to lay [my] head" (Matt 8:20), resisting pleas to stay with those I touch so that I can ever more widely tell of your kingdom and

2. Joshua 18:1 describes the ark's arrival in Shiloh. First Samuel 4:1—7:2 traces its capture, journey through Philistine territory, and resettlement in Kiriath-jearim.

> show forth your love.[3] I will bring you to Zion's "poor," feeding the hungry and healing the sick. I will bring you to Zion's "sons," confronting them with the truth and calling them to find their true sonship and their greatest triumph in me.[4] I will bring you to Zion's "priests," offering myself as the one true sacrifice. As David brought the ark of your presence to Jerusalem, I will bring myself there, though I know it will cost me my life.

Do you remember Jesus' triumphal entry, the people crying for joy as he made his way down from the Mount of Olives to the gates of the city? You will find there a recap of David's dancing procession with the ark, only now the symbols have given way to the reality. God has truly come home to his people.

IF YOUR SONS KEEP MY COVENANT . . .

There is a troubling conditionality in this psalm, and Jesus, who loves us deeply, would have felt it acutely:

> *If* your sons keep my covenant
> and my testimonies that I shall teach them,
> their sons also forever
> shall sit on your throne. (Ps 132:12)

Jesus knew of Israel's sad history since David. He knew of Solomon's idolatry at the end of his long reign, the civil war that followed, the repeated resistance to God in the divided kingdom, the long-deserved exile, and the silence of God for 450 years since Malachi.[5] He knew, in other words, that God's conditions for his continuing presence had never been met. And he knew that this would remain true to this day, with us.

Given his people's hearts and record, Jesus knew that something dramatic and unprecedented would have to happen if God was ever to come permanently and safely home to them (to us). Try again to imagine how Jesus might have made Ps 132 his own in the light of this urgent problem:

3. See Luke 4:40–44.

4. See John 8:31–47, where Jesus calls his enemies sons of the devil and calls them to the freedom of true sonship in him.

5. The sad history begins in 1 Kgs 11 and carries through to the end of the Old Testament.

> Father, "remember . . . in [my] favor," and in favor of the people you and I love, "all the hardships [I] endured" for them, how I "gave [no] sleep to my eyes," not just in Gethsemane, but all my days, until I could "find a place for [you]" among them. God of my father David, heavenly Father, "remember" what I have come to do, and when I have done it, remember it still. Remember that I have come to do what David could never do. I will do the unprecedented, the unthinkable, the undeserved. I will offer not "an ox and a fattened animal" (2 Sam 6:13) as my father David did, but I will offer myself to bring you safely home to the people you love.

When we tune our ears to hear Jesus' voice in David's words, it stirs our hearts. We meet a champion who loves us relentlessly, who will stop at nothing, who stopped at nothing, to bring God to us.

ZEALOUS FOR OUR COMPANY

There is something else that Ps 132 makes vivid. You can get at it by asking a question. Do you have a hard time feeling that God actually desires your company? He forgives you, perhaps, but does he really want you? Are you reluctant to approach God seriously because you doubt that your efforts and record, however earnest, hold much interest for him?

Tweak the language toward the end of the psalm and you will hear Jesus' comforting answer to this question:

> [You, my beloved people, are] my resting place forever;
> here [with you] I will dwell, *for I have desired it.*
> I will abundantly bless [you] . . .
> I will satisfy [you] . . .
> and [you] will shout for joy. (Ps 132:14–15, 16)

There is no reluctance in these words. They will remind you, if you let them, of Jesus' prayer the night before he gave his life for you: "Father, I *desire* that they also, whom you have given me, may be with me where I am" (John 17:24).

There was no reluctance in Jesus' choice to pour his life into the task of making a home for you with the Father. There was nothing but the longing to do whatever it would take, and whatever it will yet take, to have you safely there. Be encouraged. Be amazed.

Zealous Redeemer, there was no reluctance in your determination to have me with you. Nor is there now, even when I push you away. You have come to me, and you keep coming to me despite my reluctance, despite my unbelief, despite my resistance, to bring me to yourself at a cost that I cannot measure. You have done this because you desire me. You delight in my company, not just my praise and obedience.

Such love, such interest, calls forth my praise. It kindles my interest in you. It awakens a welcoming spirit in me. Give me the kind of delight in you and in others that you have in me. Increase my zeal to do whatever it takes to show your welcome to those around me, friend and enemy alike. Amen.

10

Contentment

Psalm 131

O LORD, my heart is not lifted up; my eyes are not raised too high; I do not occupy myself with things too great and too marvelous for me.

(Ps 131:1)

You will find it interesting and not a little confusing to read Pss 131 and 132 (the one we just looked at) back-to-back (one wonders why they were put together!). They seem to be at odds with each other. Psalm 132 is full of zeal for God's cause, while Ps 131 is about as restful as any psalm in God's songbook. Read it aloud:

> O LORD, my heart is not lifted up;
> my eyes are not raised too high;
> I do not occupy myself with things
> too great and too marvelous for me.
> But I have calmed and quieted my soul,
> like a weaned child with its mother;
> like a weaned child is my soul within me.
>
> O Israel, hope in the LORD
> from this time forth and forevermore. (Ps 131:1–3)

CONTENTMENT IN OUR LIMITS

Accepting both psalms as true, we will discover that God seems to want us to find a way to rest inwardly while we also work vigorously. As we give ourselves wholeheartedly to God's cause, we must simultaneously be like "weaned" children (Ps 131:2)—off the breast, not clamoring for their mother like baby birds, screeching and muscling each other out of the way whenever Mother approaches with a fresh worm. We must be calm, knowing that God will take care of us, even as we give our best to his cause.

When we are genuinely at rest, according to Ps 131, we are content with our limits.

> [Our] eyes are not raised too high;
> [we] do not occupy [ourselves] with things
> too great and too marvelous for [us]. (Ps 131:1)

We may be more able than others in certain areas—athletically, socially, artistically, or intellectually. But we are all creatures, and at some point each of us will hit his limit. And at that point, if our hearts are rightly aligned around a Maker who loves us, we will find contentment. At that point, our hard work will not turn into angry, frantic, or depressed work—the sort of work that reveals anger over the limits that God has imposed upon us.

We will also be content with the limits of our knowledge. William Cameron wrote, "Not everything that can be counted counts; and not everything that counts can be counted."[1] If we have found rest in God we will agree. We will not need to know the answer to every question or to have all the data. We won't need to know where the money is going to come from for our educational expenses and our hoped-for futures.

We will be content within moral constraints as well. Twice, David could have ended all his hardship by killing Saul, the crazed king who was hunting him down. But he refused to push that limit.[2] If we are finding rest in God, we will work hard for a promotion but will never lie or torpedo someone to get one. We will work hard at friendship but will never do something wrong to get someone to like us.

We will be content finally within circumstantial limits. We may have chosen, for example, to become parents—a choice that limits our present, and perhaps lifetime, career aspirations (I speak here to both fathers and mothers). If we are at rest in our "heavenly Mother" (that is the image in

1. Cameron, *Informal Sociology*, 13.
2. See 1 Sam 24:1–7 and 1 Sam 26:1–12.

v 2), we will be content to give our energies wholeheartedly to loving those children and to those perhaps now more limited tasks at work (assuming we stay at work at all). We will not frantically try to "do it all" or to "have it all."

FINDING REST WITH JESUS

David seems to have written Ps 131 on a good day. But how about the other days? How about that terrible afternoon when he pushed past the bounds of faith-filled contentment, raped another man's wife, and then had the man murdered to cover his crime?[3] How about that devastating day when, humiliated and threatened by his own son, David had to flee Jerusalem, weeping and cursed as he made his weary way?[4]

How about you? What do you do when Ps 131 feels like somebody else's song? You recall that this psalm *was* in fact somebody else's song, throughout his tumultuous life. German pastor Helmut Thielicke imagines Jesus' quiet trust in *The Waiting Father*:

> What tremendous pressures there must have been within [Jesus] to drive him to hectic, nervous, explosive activity! He sees . . . as no one else ever sees, with an infinite and awful nearness, the agony of the dying man, the prisoner's torment, the anguish of the wounded conscience, injustice, terror, dread, and beastliness. He sees and hears and feels all this with the heart of a Savior . . . Must this not fill every waking hour and rob him of sleep at night? Must he not begin immediately to set the fire burning . . . to work, work, furiously work . . . before the night comes when no man can work? That's what we would imagine the earthly life of the Son of God would be like . . .
>
> But how utterly different was the actual life of Jesus! Though the burden of the whole world lay heavy on his shoulders . . . he has time to stop and talk to the individual . . .
>
> By being obedient in his little corner of the highly provincial precincts of Nazareth and Bethlehem he allows himself to be fitted into a great mosaic whose master is God . . . And that . . . is why peace and not unrest goes out from him. For God's faithfulness

3. See 2 Sam 11.
4. See 2 Sam 15–16.

> already spans the world like a rainbow: he does not need to build it; he needs only to walk beneath it.[5]

Like David and us, Jesus had his good days and his bad days, his peaceful days and his hectic days, his days of joy and his days of misery. But through them all, he gave his heart trustingly to his Father:

> O LORD, my heart is not lifted up;
> my eyes are not raised too high . . .
> I have calmed and quieted my soul,
> like a weaned child with its mother. (Ps 131:1–2)

Jesus can give you peace if you ask him for it, for he is your brother who lived under a weight of responsibility that utterly dwarfs yours yet learned how to manage it with serenity. And his Spirit lives in you if you belong to him, ready and able to show you the way. Jesus speaks of his Spirit's ministry when he says,

> Come to me, all who labor and are heavy laden, and I will give you rest. Take my yoke upon you, and learn from me, for I am gentle and lowly in heart, and you will find rest for your souls. (Matt 11:28–29)

Ask Jesus to help you make Ps 131 more fully your song. He will.

RESTING FROM SELF-JUSTIFICATION

One additional thought. Anxiety arises not only from forces external to us but also from forces within us. Think of the treadmill of self-justification.

Have you ever found yourself having to prove that you matter, or that you are innocent, or that you are better than someone whose gifts threaten you? In all likelihood you have. And if this is so, you have found yourself pouring your energy into the hopeless task of proving what can never be proven satisfactorily. For you are, for example, rarely completely innocent, and, even if you are, people may not believe that you are, which leaves you in the same frustrating spot. And, to use another example, there will always somebody out there who is better than you are at whatever it is that you long to be really good at.

The need to justify ourselves can become so consuming that reading a "contentment" psalm like Ps 131 does not at first help us very much. We

5. See Yancey, *Church*, 94–95.

know that we need to be content with ourselves and our circumstances, but we are so unhappy with ourselves or so overwhelmed by our circumstances that it's impossible.

NOT A MIRROR BUT A PORTRAIT

What helps us push past the trap of self-justification is to stop reading Ps 131 as if it were just a mirror—a reflection of what our inner life is supposed to be like—and start reading it also as a portrait: a description of what Jesus was and is actually like, both on our behalf and inside us.

The fact that you and I can be anxious and covetous, and that our fear and envy can at times push us into behavior that rightly makes us feel ashamed, is sadly true and needs attention. But it is not our whole story. It is not even our essential story if we have met Jesus and belong to him. For if we are in Jesus, his deep and beautiful trust in the Father lives in us and covers us.

Psalm 131 is alive in you because Christ lives in you, teaching you how to rest, increasing your appetite for it, and unstoppably committed to perfecting his rest in you. And Christ also covers you (we have reflected on this once already), obscuring your fear and striving under the beauty of his perfect serenity as you struggle, drawing out God's delight and affection.

Believing that we can get off the self-justification treadmill does something very interesting. It actually increases our contentment. Reading Ps 131 as a picture of Jesus, in other words, makes it increasingly a portrait of ourselves. It makes us more like what we want to be.

Patient Redeemer, there is no mother who has ever loved her children as you love me: there is no tenderness like yours; there is no quiet endurance like yours; there is no zeal for my good like yours; there is no attentiveness like yours; there is no rest like the rest you give to me as I lean on you.

Thank you that I don't have to prove my value or innocence to you, to myself, or to anybody, for you have freely justified me. Thank you that my strivings are covered by your serenity, and that it is only a matter of time before you will perfect that serenity in me.

Quiet me by your Spirit. Fill my work with the energy of hope and joy. I ask this in your name, Lord Jesus, for you are my peace. Amen.

11

Courage
Psalm 27

The LORD is my light and my salvation; whom shall I fear?

(Ps 27:1)

In 1997 *Life is Beautiful*, now something of a classic, came to the screen. The film tells the story of an Italian man who, though not himself a Jew, chooses for love's sake to be banished to a concentration camp during WWII with his Jewish wife and little boy. He keeps his boy from being discovered and sent to his death by convincing him that the whole dreadful experience is a game and that if the boy is silent all day in the barracks (day after day), he will win an army tank when the game is over.

In one particularly courageous moment, the hero risks his life by sneaking into the office where the camp PA system is located and broadcasting the recording of a beautiful piece of music that he knows is dear to his wife. By that act he convinces her that he is still alive and that he loves her. The customary harsh commands give way briefly to great sweetness and life floods the camp. In that moment a great love issues in an act of remarkable courage. It is a beautiful moment, one that bursts upon unspeakable evil and overwhelms it.

COURAGE ARISING FROM LOVE

The film makes vivid that great courage has roots. It rises from love, in this case a man's love for his wife. The film brings to mind Ps 27, where we also find remarkable courage arising from great love, in this case love for God.

David begins the psalm declaring that nothing and no one can make him afraid:

> The LORD is my light and my salvation;
> whom shall I fear?
> The LORD is the stronghold of my life;
> of whom shall I be afraid? (Ps 27:1)

And he ends urging us to join him:

> Wait for the LORD;
> be strong, and let your heart take courage;
> wait for the LORD! (Ps 27:14)

LOVE ARISING FROM BEAUTY

A psalm like this inspires us. But it also sets us wondering, especially when we are honest about the fears that so often hamper us. How do we grow into a courageous love like this? David answers us:

> One thing have I asked of the LORD,
> that will I seek after:
> that I may dwell in the house of the LORD
> all the days of my life,
> to gaze upon the beauty of the LORD
> and to inquire in his temple. (Ps 27:4)

We might expect David to draw his strength from God's power, but he doesn't, at least not in this psalm. What enables him to stand up to "an army" (Ps 27:3) and vicious enemies like Goliath (who threatens to feed his flesh to wild animals [Ps 27:2 hints at this]) is God's beauty. David has "gaze[d]" (Ps 27:4) upon that beauty and that has made him strong. This is why he calls God his "light" (Ps 27:1), rather than his "strong arm," and it is why his heart cries out to see God's "face" (see Ps 27:8), rather than to be carried along by God's power.

GOD'S BEAUTY

God's beauty is not precisely any of the things we usually imagine when we think about God: his truth or his goodness or his love or his power. His beauty appears in these things but is not identical to them. His beauty is the quality that makes his truth, goodness, love, and power interesting and attractive. It is like the countenance of a handsome woman that becomes lovelier still when it lights up with compassion or joy.

Hebrew words for beauty describe lovers as they behold each other (Song 6:4), a particularly lovely portion of the promised land (Gen 49:15), the sound of a well-played lyre (Ps 81:2), and the taste of good bread (Prov 9:17). Beauty captures the sweet quality of David's and Jonathan's friendship (2 Sam 1:26) and the particular satisfaction that arises when "brothers dwell in unity" (Ps 133:1). It describes a well-turned gracious phrase (Prov 15:26; 16:24).

Beauty is that difficult-to-define quality that can adorn life (even in its terrible moments, as in the film) and make it worth living. It is the quality that lifts our hearts, leading us to say, "That was a beautiful gesture," or "What a beautiful relationship!" And such beauty, wherever it occurs, whether we acknowledge its origin or not, comes from God himself, whom James calls "the Father of lights," the giver of "every good gift and every perfect gift" (Jas 1:17).

BEAUTY BUILDING COURAGE

We can perhaps see something of how God's beauty worked courage for David. The boy shepherd, alone in the wilderness for innumerable long nights, had experienced God's majesty repeatedly there—in the breathtaking array of the stars and the glorious ferocity of hillside storms. David had no doubt worshiped God in these encounters, and while they had not eliminated predators, human or otherwise, those encounters had shrunk them down to size for him.

As I anticipated open-heart surgery a number of years ago, I found myself contemplating worst-case scenarios: my wife, children, and grandchildren bereft, or me living, perhaps, but severely disabled. What helped greatly was to ask myself this question: "Whatever happens, will God's beauty fade from our lives?" I knew the answer to that question was no. I knew that, one way or another, and in due time, we would all "look upon the goodness of the LORD in the land of the living" (Ps 27:13). And I knew that, in the meantime, God would remain our "light and . . . salvation" (Ps 27:1). This gave me courage.

MEETING JESUS IN PS 27

Take time now to read Ps 27 aloud in its entirety. As you do, remember that Jesus knew this psalm. Imagine him allowing David's words to give expression and shape to his heart as he made his way through life.

> The LORD is my light and my salvation;
> whom shall I fear?
> The LORD is the stronghold of my life;
> of whom shall I be afraid?
>
> When evildoers assail me
> to eat up my flesh,
> my adversaries and foes,
> it is they who stumble and fall.
>
> Though an army encamp against me,
> my heart shall not fear;
> though war arise against me,
> yet I will be confident.
>
> One thing have I asked of the LORD,
> that will I seek after:
> that I may dwell in the house of the LORD
> all the days of my life,
> to gaze upon the beauty of the LORD
> and to inquire in his temple.
>
> For he will hide me in his shelter
> in the day of trouble;
> he will conceal me under the cover of his tent;
> he will lift me high upon a rock.
>
> And now my head shall be lifted up
> above my enemies all around me,
> and I will offer in his tent
> sacrifices with shouts of joy;
> I will sing and make melody to the LORD.

Hear, O LORD, when I cry aloud;
be gracious to me and answer me!
You have said, "Seek my face."
My heart says to you,
"Your face, LORD, do I seek."
Hide not your face from me.
Turn not your servant away in anger,
O you who have been my help.
Cast me not off; forsake me not,
O God of my salvation!
For my father and my mother have forsaken me,
but the LORD will take me in.

Teach me your way, O LORD,
and lead me on a level path
because of my enemies.
Give me not up to the will of my adversaries;
for false witnesses have risen against me,
and they breathe out violence.

I believe that I shall look upon the goodness of the LORD
in the land of the living!
Wait for the LORD;
be strong, and let your heart take courage;
wait for the LORD. (Ps 27:1–14)

Jesus becomes vivid to us in these words. Early in the psalm we catch a glimpse of him when he steps forward in quiet majesty at his arrest and the mob falls back in terror:[1]

When evildoers assail me,
to eat up my flesh,
my adversaries and foes,
it is they who stumble and fall. (Ps 27:2)

We hear Jesus in verse 1 ("the Lord is my light and my salvation; whom shall I fear") when he stands before Pilate, who fancies that he holds Jesus' life and manner of death in his hands. In their final exchange Jesus at first says nothing and then softly puts him in his place: "You would have no authority over me at all unless it had been given you from above" (John 19:11).

1. See John 18:6.

The middle section of the psalm brings us to Gethsemane, where we meet Jesus yet again and begin, perhaps, to understand the deepest source of his meltdown there when we hear his repeated desperate pleading:

> Hide not your face from me.
> Turn not your servant away in anger,
> O you who have been my help.
> Cast me not off; forsake me not,
> O God of my salvation! (Ps 27:9)

What causes Jesus to collapse in horror is not just, or primarily, the physical pain that awaits him. It is the prospect of his Father's hidden "face," of being "turn[ed] . . . away in anger"—the prospect of losing the beauty of God's loving welcome as our sins come between him and the Father.

Look at verse 10:

> For my father and my mother have forsaken me,
> but the LORD will take me in. (Ps 27:10)

We don't know the story behind David's heartbreak and consolation here. But we do know that on Good Friday, there was no such consolation for Jesus. His Father did not take him in. The "light . . . of [his] life" went dark. He went to a place where David never went and where we need never go.

What does this portrait of Jesus us? It tells us that no matter how dark and difficult our story becomes, we have a Redeemer who will give us the courage we need, for he has been there himself and endured much worse.

GAZING UPON THE BEAUTY OF JESUS

There is more to see. For Jesus is not just the singer of this psalm—not just our example and our helper in the struggle to be more courageous. He is also the one about whom we sing in the psalm. He is, in other words, the source of our courage because he is himself the God of beauty, the one whom David gazed upon in the temple without knowing his name. John invites us to believe this when he tells us that in Jesus, God "became flesh and dwelt among us . . . full of grace and truth" (John 1:14).

When we see Jesus sobbing over Jerusalem's grim future, sighing over a deaf man as he heals him,[2] and gently saying, "Little girl, I say to you, arise" (Mark 5:41) to a dead twelve-year-old just before he returns her alive

2. See Luke 19:41 and Mark 7:34.

to her astonished parents, we see God. When we behold Jesus in his silent self-giving majesty as he is beaten, laughed at, spit on, and murdered, we see God in his breathtaking beauty.

We don't know what moved Victoria Leigh Soto to throw herself between the shooter and her students at Sandy Hook Elementary School on December 14, 2012, taking four bullets in the effort to spare their lives, but we do know that we see God in what she did. And seeing this God, a God who takes the deadly fire because he loves us and means for us to escape it, we witness an astonishing beauty, a beauty that helps us to stand more firmly against what is wrong in ourselves and our world.

Take a moment to find and play a video of "Fairest Lord Jesus" and sing along. Call to mind as you do that to call Jesus "fairest" is to say that he is more beautiful than anything else that you might hold dear. Reflect particularly on the beauty of the love that brought him to die for you and worship him for that love. It will make you more courageous.

God, you are beautiful. You are interesting, creative, and attractive, and you mean for me to enjoy you in the beautiful things of life. You love it when I laugh, when my heart warms in a gathering of friends, when a tree or a sunrise or a soaring creature or a piece of music takes my breath away.

Lord Jesus, you have brought God's beauty to me more clearly and more vividly than any of his good gifts could. You make him interesting and attractive to me. In you I see God loving children, singing with friends, enhancing the wine at a wedding, feeding hungry people, restoring a dead child to her parents, seeking out those whom no one wants to be with, and standing up to bullies I would cower before. In you I see God choosing things I would never willingly choose—hunger, thirst, poverty, loneliness, and every other misery of life. In you I see him choosing to be stripped, beaten, spit upon, laughed at, tortured, and murdered in solidarity with those who suffer these cruelties. I see him choosing to be desolate, without comfort and hope, as he passed for my sake out of heaven's welcome into a darkness that I will never have to experience.

Open my eyes more fully to the richness of your goodness toward me. Make that goodness so attractive to me that it shrinks the hard things in my life down to manageable size. Make it so attractive to me that I find it taking firmer root in me, making me a more courageous person. Make my love deeper and laughter stronger. Amen.

12

Confessing

Psalm 32

I said, "I will confess my transgressions to the LORD,"
and you forgave the iniquity of my sin.
(Ps 32:5)

HOW DO WE MEET Jesus in a psalm of confession? He had no sins to confess, so are we alone, stuck solely with ourselves, when we read, "Against you, you only, have I sinned" (Ps 51:4), or when we celebrate forgiveness, as happens in Ps 32? No. We can find Jesus in such places as well. Let's first hear our own voices in Ps 32, and then we will reflect on how to encounter Jesus there.

FRIGHTENING SOLITUDE

Columnist Kate Murphy reports the following findings of University of Virginia psychology professor Timothy Wilson: "In 11 experiments involving more than 700 people, the majority of participants reported that they found it unpleasant to be alone in a room with their thoughts for just 6–15 minutes." Murphy comments,

> If there is ever a still moment for reflective thought, say, while waiting in line at the grocery store or sitting in traffic, out comes the cell phone.[1]

We are not all this way, to be sure. Some of us relish solitude. Some of us might not even own cell phones! Still, Murphy is on to something. There are dark and confusing realities in each of us that we would rather not face. Among them are matters that trouble our consciences, attitudes and choices that we know to be wrong. Some of them are just below the surface of our consciousness, just waiting for a moment of solitude to express themselves; many are more deeply buried because we don't have the skill or inclination to deal with them (Jeremiah writes, "The heart is deceitful above all things, and desperately sick; who can understand it?" [Jer 17:9].)

THE RELIEF OF COMING CLEAN

One strategy often used for dealing with a bad conscience is to keep busy so that we don't have to face ourselves. Psalm 32 offers an alternative strategy, a refreshing and ultimately transformational one: tell the truth about what is amiss. It's OK and life-changing, in other words, to be honest.

> Blessed is the one whose transgression is forgiven,
> whose sin is covered.
> Blessed is the man against whom the LORD counts no iniquity,
> and in whose spirit there is no deceit.
>
> For when I kept silent, my bones wasted away
> through my groaning all day long.
> For day and night your hand was heavy upon me;
> my strength was dried up as by the heat of summer.
> I acknowledged my sin to you,
> and I did not cover my iniquity;
> I said, "I will confess my transgressions to the LORD,"
> and you forgave the iniquity of my sin.
>
> Therefore let everyone who is godly
> offer prayer to you at a time when you may be found;
> surely in the rush of great waters,
> they shall not reach him.
> You are a hiding place for me;

1. Murphy, "No Time," 3. Citing Wilson, "Just Think," 75.

you preserve me from trouble;
you surround me with shouts of deliverance.

I will instruct you and teach you in the way you should go;
I will counsel you with my eye upon you.
Be not like a horse or a mule, without understanding,
which must be curbed with bit and bridle,
or it will not stay near you.

Many are the sorrows of the wicked,
but steadfast love surrounds the one who trusts in the LORD.
Be glad in the LORD, and rejoice, O righteous,
and shout for joy, all you upright in heart! (Ps 32:1–11)

We find at least two reasons for honesty in these words. The first reason is that hiding makes us miserable:

For when I kept silent, my bones wasted away
through my groaning all day long.
For day and night your hand was heavy upon me;
my strength was dried up as by the heat of summer.
(Ps 32:3–4)

Our troubled consciences can exhaust us, even when we deny our guilt. They can be like chronic pain, after us day and night and never letting up. Lady Macbeth tries unsuccessfully to cope by scrubbing her hands while she sleepwalks, muttering,

Out damned spot! Out, I say! . . .
Here's the smell of blood still. All the perfumes of Arabia will not sweeten this little hand. Oh, oh, oh![2]

Making excuses, spinning our stories so that we look better than we actually are, can be a full-time job. Only facing the truth can bring relief.

THE WAY TO JOY

The second reason for coming clean is that it opens the way to joy. We sometimes think that confession is a final destination to which we must drag ourselves, spurred on by the notion that God's chief aim is for us to

2. Shakespeare, "MACBETH," V.i lines 32, 47–48, 1131.

feel terrible about ourselves. But Ps 32 denies this emphatically, as it opens and when it ends:

> Blessed [happy, joyfully relieved] is the one whose transgression is
> forgiven [literally, "lifted" off his back],
> whose sin is covered [literally, "buried" or "hidden away"].
> (Ps 32:1)

> Be glad in the LORD, and rejoice, O righteous,
> and shout for joy. (Ps 32:11)

David isn't wearing a long face and dark clothes as he confesses.

Certainly there will be times when we grieve deeply over something we have done, and perhaps even more profoundly over discovering the sorts of people we are, as is made vivid by our behavior. But while grief may accompany confession, it is not what God is after in the end. He means for honesty to set us free. Confession, in God's plan, is a doorway into life and love and joy.

THE WAY TO GOD

Why does confession open the way to joy? Because it opens the way to God, and fellowship with him is what we were designed for. God himself reminds us of this by abruptly interrupting the psalmist halfway through the psalm. Up to this moment David has been speaking. Now God does:

> I will instruct you and teach you in the way you should go;
> I will counsel you with my eye upon you.
> Be not like a horse or a mule, without understanding,
> which must be curbed with bit and bridle,
> or it will not stay near you. (Ps 32:8–9)

God isn't interested in "mules without understanding" whom he has to jerk around with "bit and bridle," forcing you and me through circumstances we don't understand so that we don't harm ourselves or mess up his world. He wants children to talk to, learners who will engage with him and, in the context of that engagement, make good choices.

We hear Jesus' warm welcome in these words, for he calls to us in a very similar way in the gospel:

> Come to *me* [not to some perfectionist self-improvement plan—nor to some lonely place of self-hatred], all who labor and are

> heavy laden, and I will give you rest. Take my yoke upon you, and learn from me [*let me teach you*], for I am gentle and lowly in heart, and you will find rest for your souls. (Matt 11:28–29)

To confess is to stop running away. It is to stop hiding from God like Adam and Eve did after their sin. It is to turn around and to face the Person who seeks us and wants us. And it is to hear God say, surprisingly, "It's OK. Come on home. Rest. Learn."

People may want the truth so that they can bully us or gloat over us. But God never does. He wants the truth (the truth he already knows, by the way) because he wants *us*.

EMBEDDED PROBLEM

There is a problem embedded in what I have just been saying. It is a problem lurking in Ps 32, and if we have tender consciences, we will recognize it. It is a problem that only Jesus can fix.

Let me illustrate. Imagine that you have just been pulled over for texting while driving. The officer asks,

> It looks like you were texting. Were you?
>
> Yes, indeed, officer, I was texting. You caught me red-handed. And, of course, now that I have openly admitted it, I'm free to go—right? You owe me forgiveness because I have been honest, right?

What is the officer going to do? It is very unlikely that he is going to let you off. If he has had a bad day, he might even look for something extra to nail you on since you are such a smart aleck. Your argument makes no sense. To admit to the texting is the most likely way to guarantee a ticket. The best way not to get a summons is denial.

If you confess an affair to your wife, she may forgive you. But she does not owe you forgiveness because you have confessed. She might just as well, and with biblical warrant, end the marriage.

CORRELATION AND CAUSATION

My wife (speaking of wives) is a scientist, and she is fond of pointing out to her students that "correlation does not imply causation." The fact that two events happen at the same time or in the same place or under a similar set of circumstances does not tell us anything at all about the causal relationship between those two events. The fact that our confessing and God's open-hearted welcome are correlated in Ps 32 does not at all mean that the one causes the other.

Here is an additional problem. Even if confession somehow earned forgiveness, ours would not because we don't confess very well. Even at our most honest moments, we don't tell God everything, if for no other reason than that we cannot or will not see everything. In addition, we are rarely sufficiently sorry. I can think of times when my wife has nailed me about something (she rarely does this—but there have been occasions), and I have petulantly cried, "OK! I admit it! I was wrong! And you were right! AGAIN!" What kind of confession is that? It certainly does not restore fellowship. It only makes the problem worse.

So, how can the correlation between your honesty and God's welcoming forgiveness be true? How can you have any confidence that confessing will open the way to his embrace? Perhaps, for some odd reason, it happened with David, but why should it happen with you or me?

MEETING JESUS

We can hope for forgiveness because of the deeper story to which Ps 32, together with all the psalms, belongs—the story of the God who fully joined us in our humanity.

Try an experiment. Imagine Jesus reading verses 3–4 aloud as a young man, say when he was twenty-one, and thinking about one of his brothers, or his mother, or you, as he read:

> For when I kept silent, my bones wasted away
> through my groaning all day long.
> For day and night your hand was heavy upon me;
> my strength was dried up as by the heat of summer.
> (Ps 32:3–4)

What would have run through Jesus' heart and mind as he thought of people he loved? Surely the same sort of thing that runs through a mother as she watches a child make poor choices, deny them, and begin to reap their sad consequences. A longing would have risen in him that his "children" would somehow escape those consequences. And along with that longing, there would have arisen questions:

How, Father, will they escape? What must I do so that they can?

And with those questions would have come the growing conviction that he must somehow trade places with them (with us).

TRADING PLACES FULLY

Hearing Jesus' voice in Ps 32 opens us to the discovery of how fully Jesus traded places with us. He chose not simply to identify with our sins. He also chose to experience what sin does to us if we linger in it. He chose to feel God's "heavy" hand (Ps 32:4), like you and I do when we are hiding from the truth. He chose to feel the burning "heat of summer" (Ps 32:4), what comes to us when unrelieved guilt exhausts us. We say, sometimes too glibly, "I feel your pain." God says this as well and means it.

I keep saying that there are multiple voices in the psalms—our voices, the psalmists' voices, and the voice of Jesus. But you need also to see that there is a mysterious sense in which there is just one voice—the voice of a blended song. For God has put you and me together with Jesus, and he has put Jesus together with us. Jesus has taken the full package of human misery and failure—not just the guilt of our sin but also the miseries that our sins cause us. He has even taken on our flawed confessions. And he has embraced the whole package so that we can take on his cries of confident hope as our own.

WHY CONFESSING WORKS

I hope you are beginning to see how the link between our honesty and God's welcome works. That link does not lie in our honesty. It does not lie in how well we confess or how sorry we feel for what we have done wrong. It lies in the choice God made to annihilate our dark story in all its parts by entering it in all its parts—not just owning our sin as if it were his but enduring the physical, spiritual, and social impacts of our sin as if he deserved them. Isaiah tells us that "with his wounds we are healed" (Isa 53:5). Those wounds include the physical and psychological impacts of sin, impacts that Ps 32 describes so vividly, impacts that Jesus chose to endure for our sakes.

So it is truly safe—it is in fact liberating and exhilarating—for you to come clean with God. It is safe and freeing even for you to say, "Lord, I am sure that what I am trying to admit to you involves all sorts of things I am not yet able or willing to admit." It is safe because coming clean puts you into Christ, where God's welcome always abounds.

Listen and you will hear Jesus' speaking to God on your behalf in verses 6–7:

> Therefore, let everyone who is godly
> offer prayers to you at a time when you may be found;
> surely in the rush of great waters [that flood of accusation that
> drags their bodies and souls down],
> they shall not reach him.
> You are a hiding place for [them]. (Ps 32:6–7)

To be "godly" (v 6) is not, happily, to be perfect. But it is to be inclined toward God rather than away from him. It is to be as honest as we can be. And to be that sort of person is to find yourself "hiding" (v 7) in God, all wrapped up and safe in Jesus' moral beauty, on your way out of the suffocating grip of your old life and self. God himself, coming to us in Jesus, it turns out, is the cause of the correlation between our honesty and the relief of his certain and enduring welcome.

SHOUTS OF DELIVERANCE

Notice one last thing before we leave Ps 32. Notice the jubilation. Have you ever found it difficult to believe that God is glad to see you again—say, when you have had to admit to the same sin for what feels like the hundredth time? Have you ever said to yourself, "I suppose he will forgive me—after all, he promises to. But I doubt it will be with arms as widely open as the first time. He has got to be tired of me by now."

Psalm 32 says "no!" to such thoughts, and it helps us feel that "no!" in verse 7:

> You are a hiding place for me;
> you preserve me from trouble;
> you surround me with *shouts of deliverance*. (Ps 32:7)

Those "shouts of deliverance" may well include those of our friends who gladly welcome us back when we come clean. But they are essentially God's own shouts, heard by Zephaniah as he foresees God's jubilation over Israel's forgiveness and final restoration:

> Sing aloud, O daughter of Zion . . .
> The Lord has taken away the judgments against you . . .

He will rejoice over you with gladness;
    he will quiet you with his love;
he will exalt over you with loud singing. (Zeph 3:14, 15, 17)[3]

Jesus picks up this song, making God's jubilation his own as he brings us home on his shoulders:

> What man of you, having a hundred sheep, if he has lost one of them, does not leave the ninety-nine in the open country, and go after the one that is lost, until he finds it? And when he has found it, he lays it on his shoulders, rejoicing. And when he comes home, he calls together his friends and his neighbors, saying to them, "Rejoice with me, for I have found my sheep that was lost." (Luke 15:4–6)

So turn to the Good Shepherd. Be honest about what is wrong and let him carry you home. Rejoice in the gladness of his welcome. And keep doing so.

Glorious things of thee are spoken,
Zion, city of our God;
He whose Word cannot be broken
Formed thee for his own abode:
On the Rock of ages founded,
Who can shake thy sure repose?
With salvation's walls surrounded,
Thou may'st smile on all thy foes.[4]

Tender Shepherd and faithful Guide, how heartening it is to know that you welcome my confessions. You don't just put up with me when I come clean, even when it is over and over again for the same failing. You sing out with shouts of joy and call upon the whole of heaven to rejoice with you. You do this even though my confessions lack completeness, even when my confessions are reluctant and half-hearted. You respond as you do because you delight in my fellowship and because you long to see me free from the damage that unrelieved guilt does to me—to my body, to

3. By the time Zephaniah prophesied in Jerusalem (not long after 640 BC), the unrepentant Northern Kingdom was a distant and tragic memory—destroyed and transported by the Assyrians a hundred years prior. And Jerusalem under Manasseh and Amon (696–40 BC) had been courting a similar fate, embracing as a vassal of Assyria its moral and religious corruptions, including human sacrifice. Consequently, much of Zephaniah predicts God's judgment on Judah, Jerusalem and the nations. Starting at Zeph 3:9, the message abruptly changes as Zephaniah foresees God intervening to convert, forgive, and restore his people and the world.

4. Newton, "Glorious Things," 345.

my inner person, and to my relationships. You respond as you do, despite all the imperfections that compromise my communications with you, because you have carried my guilt in your body and soul is if it were yours, bearing it away from me forever.

There is no one who loves me like you do. There is no one who has endured what you endured to bring me safely home. Send your Spirit to convince me ever more deeply of how safe I am. By his reassurance make me more honest with you and with others. I pray in your welcoming and jubilant name. Amen.

13

Suffering

Psalm 69

My eyes grow dim with waiting for my God. More in number than the hairs of my head are those who hate me without cause.

(Ps 69:3–4)

One of the reasons we love the psalms is that they often resonate with us when we are going through hard times. Job's comforters do not comfort him very much. They give him theories, and even blame him, in the effort to explain his suffering. But the psalms simply enter our sufferings with us, authenticating them in words that are often much better than those we can come up with.

WORDS TO HELP US IN HARD TIMES

Sometimes we grow deeply discouraged in our efforts to help loved ones reconcile. On such occasions, it is consoling to know that we are not alone:

> Too long have I had my dwelling
> among those who hate peace.
> I am for peace,
> but when I speak, they are for war! (Ps 120:6–7)

Often, when we are depressed, yesterday's joy feels like a mirage. At such times we find companionship and hope in Ps 126:

> When the LORD restored the fortunes of Zion,
> we were like those who dream.
> Then [*but not now*] our mouth was filled with laughter,
> and our tongue with shouts of joy;
> then they said among the nations,
> "The LORD has done great things for them" . . .
> Restore our fortunes, O LORD,
> like streams in the Negeb!
> Those who sow in tears
> shall reap with shouts of joy! (Ps 126:1–2, 4–5)

There are times when the cruelty of others so demoralizes and exhausts us that all we can do is cry:

> Be gracious to me, O LORD, for I am languishing;
> heal me, O LORD, for my bones are troubled . . .
> I am weary with my moaning;
> every night I flood my bed with tears;
> I drench my couch with my weeping. (Ps 6:2, 6)

Sometimes a sense of isolation overwhelms us:

> Look to the right and see:
> there is none who takes notice of me;
> no refuge remains to me;
> no one cares for my soul. (Ps 142:4)

There are times when we have sincerely sought to do the right thing, and all we get for our efforts is indifference, or even cruel rejection:

> All in vain have I kept my heart clean
> and washed my hands in innocence. (Ps 73:13)

How consoling and refreshing to find such words in God's book! The psalms give us permission to say the sorts of things we might be reluctant to say in church. They invite us to break through the facades that can make the Christian life so lonely.

JESUS' VOICE

But don't forget what I have been saying: we do not read any of these passages sufficiently if the only voice we hear in them is our own. We must keep telling ourselves that there are other voices speaking as well, most notably the voice of Jesus, whose suffering runs deeper than ours (especially because it was never deserved), to places we will never have to go if we belong to him.

The following excerpt from Ps 69 omits the personal and cosmic jubilation with which the psalm ends. But it is the part that we need to examine for the purposes of this chapter. Read it aloud, listening especially for the voice of Jesus.

> Save me, O God!
> For the waters have come up to my neck.
> I sink in deep mire,
> where there is no foothold;
> I have come into deep waters,
> and the flood sweeps over me.
> I am weary with my crying out;
> my throat is parched.
> My eyes grow dim
> with waiting for my God.
>
> More in number than the hairs of my head
> are those who hate me without cause;
> mighty are those who would destroy me,
> those who attack me with lies.
> What I did not steal
> must I now restore?
> O God, you know my folly;
> the wrongs I have done are not hidden from you.
>
> Let not those who hope in you be put to shame through me,
> O Lord GOD of hosts;
> let not those who seek you be brought to dishonor through me,
> O God of Israel.
> For it is for your sake that I have borne reproach,
> that dishonor has covered my face.
> I have become a stranger to my brothers,
> an alien to my mother's sons.

For zeal for your house has consumed me,
        and the reproaches of those who reproach you have fallen
            on me . . .
I am the talk of those who sit in the gate,
        and the drunkards make songs about me . . .

Hide not your face from your servant;
        for I am in distress; make haste to answer me . . .

Reproaches have broken my heart,
        so that I am in despair.
I looked for pity, but there was none,
        and for comforters, but I found none.
They gave me poison for food,
        and for my thirst they gave me sour wine to drink.
        (Ps 69:1–9, 12, 17, 20–21)

It is hard to hear Jesus in verse 5 ("O God, you know my folly; the wrongs I have done are not hidden from you"). But it takes little imagination to hear him everywhere else.

MULTI-DIMENSIONAL SUFFERING

The suffering here is multi-dimensional, coming at our Lord like arrows from a surrounding enemy. He is hated by those who are bitter at God about their lives but don't know how to blame God (or are afraid to), so they take it out on him:

> The reproaches of those who reproach you have fallen on me. (Ps 69:9)

He endures injustice, paying a debt he doesn't owe:

What I did not steal,
        must I now restore? (Ps 69:4)

Jesus suffers cruel and public ridicule:

I am the talk of those who sit at the gate [those with social power],
        and the drunkards make songs about me. (Ps 69:12)

What political attack ads have done to candidates and social media trolls may have done to you or your children, Jesus' enemies do to him. After his condemnation, nameless Roman guards make Jesus look ridiculous, dressing his battered body in a royal robe and bowing before him, beating his blindfolded face and ordering him to prophecy, spitting on him, offering him bitter wine as his thirst torments him:

> For my thirst they gave me sour wine to drink. (Ps 69:21)

To complete Jesus' humiliation, they strip him of his one remaining garment, and as he hangs naked and dying, religious leaders and strangers laugh at his helplessness, inviting him with sneers to come down from the cross: we can almost hear them "mak[ing] songs" (Ps 69:12) about him: "He saved others; he cannot save himself . . . He trusts in God; let God deliver him now, if he desires him" (Matt 27:42, 43).

FRIENDLESS

More painful certainly than the ridicule of his enemies is the isolation from his friends:

> I have become a stranger to my brothers. (Ps 69:8)

Robert Frost famously wrote, "Home is the place where, when you have to go there, they have to take you in."[1] But Jesus seems not to have known that welcome as his public ministry heated up. His family had tried to curtail his ministry by force, and as he breathed his last, the only "brother" to whom Jesus could commend his mother for care was the disciple John.[2]

Jesus' new family became those who "do the will of God": they are "my brother and sister and mother" (Mark 3:35). But even they left him in one way or another. Peter rebuked him when he said he had to die in Jerusalem ("Reproaches have broken my heart" [Ps 69:20]: did Jesus' angry outburst arise from a broken heart?). And in his final hours, when he needed friends the most, he could only say, "I looked for pity, but there was none, and for comforters, but I found none" (Ps 69:20).

Remember Judas' stealthy departure from the Last Supper. Remember Jesus in the garden, prostrate, facing the most terrible moment in his life, as his disciples slept. Remember him a little later as his disciples fled before the arresting mob.[3] Remember Peter's ferocious denial: "Then he began to invoke a curse on himself and to swear, 'I do not know the man'" (Matt

1. Frost, "Death," 20.
2. See Mark 3:21 and John 19:26–27.
3. See John 13:27–30, Matt 26:36–46, and Matt 26:56.

26:74). Remember Jesus, alone, facing the mob as they chose Barabbas over him and then shouted repeatedly, "Let him be crucified!" (Matt 27:22).

SUFFERING AT GOD'S HAND

Jesus greatest suffering happens at God's hand. When the psalmist cries, "Hide not your face from [me]" (Ps 69:17), he only feels that God is absent—as it is with us in our bleakest moments. But when Jesus pleads in the garden of Gethsemane, "Father . . . remove this cup from me!" (Mark 14:36), the desertion is real—or will soon be. Jesus was the truest servant of God who has ever lived, the one who did not simply "do things *for* God" but who "did everything *with* God." Fellowship with the Father was the heartbeat of his life. But at the cross, he let go of all that: he chose outer darkness, deepest rejection, hell itself.

The closest parallel to this in our experience is the sundering of a really good friendship, or divorce after years of a strong marriage. For such a rift to happen is to have the heart ripped out of one's life. This analogy, of course, goes only so far, for we have never known, even in our best friendships, the quality of relationship that was broken as Jesus perished in the darkness. We feel the devastation of Jesus' isolation in the psalmist's opening cries:

> Save me, O God!
> For the waters have come up to my neck.
> I sink in deep mire,
> where there is no foothold;
> I have come into deep waters,
> and the flood sweeps over me.
> I am weary with my crying out;
> my throat is parched.
> My eyes grow dim
> with waiting for my God. (Ps 69:1–3)

It is reported that one of the great horrors in the trench warfare of the First World War was mud so thick and deep that soldiers who fell off the scaffolding in the trenches could, and did, drown in the muck. Jesus is drowning in his anguish: it is up to his neck, and there is no place to set his feet. And the suffering is unrelieved. He is all prayed out ("I am weary with my crying out" [Ps 69:3]), he has no tears left, and yet he is still alone in his torment.

We can begin to understand why, in the midst of the darkness on Good Friday, Jesus cried out, "My God, my God, why have you forsaken me?" (Mark 15:34). Unlike the psalmist, Jesus knew what was happening, he knew why, and he had the promise that all would be well in the end. But the horror was so terrible that it eclipsed all that knowledge. His "zeal for [God's] house" had brought him to the place where, like a burnt offering of old, he was utterly "consumed" (Ps 69:9), body and soul.

NOT THEM!

Perhaps the most moving words of the psalm, when we hear Jesus in them, are the ones we find in verse 6.

> Let not those who hope in you be put to shame through me. (Ps 69:6)

They make us think of Jesus' words at his arrest: "I told you [he says to the mob] that I am he. So, if you seek me, *let these men go* [Don't drag them into this!]" (John 18:8).

Soon to face the fulness of degradation and desolation we have been describing, Jesus thinks only of us, issuing a fierce directive that distances us from his shame and suffering. Like a loving parent accused of some terrible crime, he directs his enemies not to let his family be dragged by association into his shame. What an astonishing friend we have!

BRINGING HIS SHIFT OUT

In August of 2010 an explosion in a Chilean mine buried thirty-three workers deep beneath the surface. For sixty-nine days, rescuers labored around the clock to drill a 28-inch diameter hole from the surface to the miners a half-mile below as families, friends, and co-workers anxiously waited and prayed. Shortly after midnight on October 13, the first captive emerged, followed over the next twenty-two hours by all the others. The last to break the surface was the crew's foreman, Luis Urzua, who had chosen to remain below until all his men had escaped the ordeal. Chilean President Sebastián Pinera was on hand to embrace and greet him: "You brought your shift out like a good captain."

What a vivid glimpse Mr. Urzua gives us of Jesus, joining us in our suffering until the last of us is delivered. There are differences, of course, that make Jesus' suffering even more wondrous. Urzua was already underground when the mine collapsed, whereas Jesus was safe aboveground and chose to descend. Urzua suffered with his crew, whereas Jesus suffered not only *with* us but *for* us. And Urzua made it out, whereas Jesus perished at the bottom of the shaft to guarantee our deliverance.

Still, the parallel moves and encourages me, as I suspect it does you. No matter how far down we may find ourselves, Jesus is there with us. He knows our sufferings because he is with us in the midst of them as a fellow sufferer, even still.[4] And he will never leave us. He will see us through the darkest times until they are over.

Psalm 69 ends in jubilation, making me think of the joy that greeted those Chilean miners as they emerged from the ground. Imagine Jesus singing at your side when all is said and done. Imagine you and the cosmos joining in. This will happen.

> I will praise the name of God with a song;
> I will magnify him with thanksgiving . . .
> For the LORD hears the needy
> and does not despise his own people who are prisoners.
> Let heaven and earth praise him,
> the seas and everything that moves in them.
> For God will save Zion. (Ps 69:30, 33–35)

Lord Jesus, I wonder at your choice to share human shame and suffering so fully with us. Thank you that you know what it feels like to be falsely accused, to be ridiculed, and to be viciously hated. Thank you that you know what it feels like to suffer ravenous thirst and to be without friends when you need them the most. Thank you that you know what it feels like to die without the comfort of your Father.

You chose this solidarity with us to lift us from the shame, loss, and suffering that fill our story. When you told your captors to "let these others go," it was as if you were speaking to your Father on our behalf. You chose the shame that you did not deserve in order to lift us out of the shame that we deserve and into the honor that you left behind when you joined us here. You chose to be falsely accused to rescue us from the

4. When, after his resurrection, Jesus confronts Saul on the Damascus road for persecuting the church, he says, "Saul, Saul, why are you persecuting *me*" (Acts 9:4). Jesus' suffering as our sin-bearer is over. But his engagement with our sorrows otherwise continues.

accusations that are rightly made against us. You chose to be viciously hated to rescue us from the world in which we are both the hated ones and the ones who hate. You died without the Father so that we can die with him.

I know this story, but I would be foolish to think I could measure its worth. I confess that I am capable of an appalling indifference to what you have done for me. Forgive my cold heart, gracious Savior, by the merits of the cross. Mighty Spirit, open the eyes of my heart to the dimensions of your love. Heavenly Father, silence my complaining, and shake heaven and earth with your praises. Amen.

14

Betrayed

Psalm 55

For it is not an enemy who taunts me—then I could bear it . . . But it is you, a man, my equal, my companion, my familiar friend.

(Ps 55:12, 13)

Betrayal is arguably the most exquisite pain that we endure. It is hard enough when an enemy treats us cruelly. But when a spouse or close friend turns upon us, using their intimate knowledge of us (knowledge they have acquired because we trusted them enough to be vulnerable) to wound us, it can be unbearable.

The Gospel writers tell us that Judas betrayed Jesus. We know the story. We perhaps have noted with sorrow the terrible doom that Jesus pronounces upon his friend, and we may even have wondered at Jesus' mysterious ability to see into Judas' heart and plans. But in all likelihood, we have not thought about how Judas' betrayal hurt Jesus.

For some reason we have allowed ourselves to forget, or never adequately to appreciate, that Jesus was fully our brother. We have allowed ourselves to believe that because Jesus was divine and knew what was coming, the human side of his experience was not quite as painful to him as it would be to us. But this is a mistake, and it robs us of the enormous comfort of knowing that he "gets" betrayal from deeply within its devastating fullness. He "gets" it even more wrenchingly than we do, not only because it led to his death, but also because his love for Judas was greater than our love for our friends: the greater the love, the greater the pain when it is betrayed.

FEELING JESUS' PAIN

Sections of Ps 55 help us feel Jesus' pain. Read the following aloud, listening for Jesus' voice.

> My heart is in anguish within me;
> the terrors of death have fallen upon me.
> Fear and trembling come upon me,
> and horror overwhelms me.
> And I say, "Oh, that I had wings like a dove!
> I would fly away and be at rest;
> yes, I would wander far away;
> I would lodge in the wilderness;
> I would hurry to find a shelter
> from the raging wind and tempest" . . .
>
> For it is not an enemy who taunts me—
> then I could bear it;
> it is not an adversary who deals insolently with me—
> then I could hide from him.
> But it is you, a man, my equal,
> my companion, my familiar friend.
> We used to take sweet counsel together;
> within God's house we walked in the throng . . .
>
> My companion stretched out his hand against his friends;
> he violated his covenant.
> His speech was smooth as butter,
> yet war was in his heart;
> his words were softer than oil,
> yet they were drawn swords. (Ps 55:4–8, 12–14, 20–21)

The devastation in these words likely arises from more than betrayal (as we read them, we encounter Jesus in the Garden of Gethsemane crying out to be delivered from the coming hell of the cross). But betrayal is woven into the horror. The psalmist is desperate to flee the voice of the one who taunts him ("I would fly away" [Ps 55:6]) because he was once "my equal, my companion, my familiar friend" (Ps 55:13). He is pierced by the memories of "sweet counsel together . . . within God's house" (Ps 55:14).

CHOSEN PAIN

You have perhaps experienced betrayal. If you have, you know that it came unchosen and unsought. Jesus' story is different. He chose betrayal, his eyes wide open to it before it happened. He made that choice, not because he desired it but because he desired even more to share our experience with us. Jesus refused to take an end-run around our pain because he loves us and he knew that the only way to deliver us from it was to endure it. This is one of the mysteries of the gospel story: by absorbing evil, our Maker somehow removes it.

Jesus chose to endure betrayal for another reason. He and the Father wanted us to see what has been going on for a long time. God's sufferings over our many betrayals did not begin with Judas and the terrible cross that followed; they only culminated there. The psalmist gives voice in Ps 55 to the grief of the God who told Hosea to marry and stay faithful to a faithless woman, so that we would begin to understand what our many betrayals cost him:

> Go again, love a woman who is loved by another man and is an adulteress, even as the LORD loves the children of Israel, though they turn to other gods and love cakes of raisins. (Hos 3:1)

Our religious wanderings are ancient and continual—and outrageous (we prefer "cakes" to God!). And God has never been indifferent to them. They have hurt him and continue to hurt him in the same way that cheating and betrayal hurt us.

IS GOD REALLY HURTABLE?

Do you have a hard time thinking of God as "hurtable"? Isn't God far above us—sovereign and majestic? Is he not independent of us, not needing us the way we need him? Yes, God is all of these things. He is much more than a woundable friend. But he is not less than a woundable friend. When at the very start he made us "in his image" (like him and for him), God arranged the spiritual cosmos so that he could be relationally woundable, so that we could actually "grieve the Holy Spirit" (Eph 4:30).

We may know this abstractly. But Ps 55, when we hear Jesus' voice in it, helps us feel it. It reveals God's heart to us. And it opens the way to similar discoveries throughout the psalms, as in Ps 69:

> Reproaches have *broken my heart*,
> so that I am in despair.
> I looked for pity, but there was none,
> and for comforters, but I found none. (Ps 69:20)

HIGHLY VALUED

As we begin to get a feeling for how God feels, we begin to discover something so remarkable that it can leave us speechless. We begin to discover how profoundly God values us. We can take no credit for that value: it is the gift of his grace at our creation, confirmed by the gift of himself in our redemption.[1] Nevertheless it is real. For if we did not matter to him in some essential, soul-stirring way, we could not possibly hurt him as much as he tells us we do.

We are not, it turns out, like pet hamsters, whose bite can be a nuisance but little more. We are made in God's image, like children before their father, and our bite can break God's heart, like the perceived ingratitude of King Lear's daughter broke his: May she feel, he cries,

> How sharper than a serpent's tooth it is
> To have a thankless child.[2]

NOT DEPRIVED

Have you ever wished you could have *been* Matthew or John, rather than simply having their Gospels to read? Have you ever wished you could have been there, on the spot, able to interact with God-in-the-flesh, to feel his joys and pains, to pick up the inflection in his voice, to sense what was

1. God chose to create us in his image, reflecting his own nobility and love in our relationship to him and to each other (see Gen 1:26–27). He chose to honor us further by taking our humanity fully upon himself when "the Word became flesh and dwelt among us" (John 1:14). And he confirmed our value to him by giving himself up for us, so that "he might present the church to himself in splendor, without spot or wrinkle or any such thing" (Eph 5:27).

2. Shakespeare, "King Lear," Act I, Scene IV, lines 279–80, 1073.

going on inside him? Have you ever with regret told yourself that you have only the smallest portion of what the disciples had?

If you have had such regrets, you need to adjust your thinking. For you have the psalms—not just Ps 55, but all of them. And, along with them, you have the Spirit of Christ who is both in them and in you. If you listen carefully, you will encounter Jesus there at least as fully as the disciples did, perhaps more fully. You will meet him in the weight of his grief, the ferocity of his anger, the purity of his love, and the intensity of his joy over you. And meeting Jesus more fully, you will meet God more fully, for Jesus said, "Whoever has seen me has seen the Father" (John 14:9).

You are not deprived at all!

Lord Jesus, did Judas's betrayal hurt you so deeply that you wanted to flee from it like a dove on the wing? Was it for you like a raging tempest in your heart? Did it grieve you inconsolably, recalling at the Last Supper the times of earnest discussion you had had with Judas and knowing now that he was absent because he was securing your arrest? For me to say no to these questions is for me to deny that you were fully human, tested in every way as I am. For me to say yes to them is to discover that God is woundable, for you said that we see what he is like when we look at you.

To believe that Judas broke your heart is to believe that I do too. For you love me as you loved him. Thanks to your Holy Spirit, you are with me, caring for me, teaching me, warning me, feeding me, loving me through the people you send my way.

And yet, like Judas, I make light of your love. I praise you on Sunday and ignore you on Wednesday. I betray you with indifference and distrust, with anger and fear, with denials and deceit, and with disobedience and cruelty. Make me genuinely sorry for wounding you so persistently. Warm my heart toward you through the forgiveness of your cross and the filling of your Spirit. Amen.

15

Delivered

Psalm 116

You have delivered my soul from death, my eyes from tears, my feet from stumbling; I will walk before the LORD in the land of the living.

(Ps 116:8–9)

In the summer of 2013, my wife and I left for weeklong family reunion in another part of the country, knowing that I had a large growth on one of my kidneys but not knowing what it was. Rollicking in a pool one afternoon with one of our granddaughters proved particularly poignant when I found myself wondering how many more moments like this were in store. I recalled how only a few years earlier, a close friend had died of kidney cancer, leaving his family bereft. Why shouldn't that be my story as well?

Upon our return, we arranged immediately for tests, and after they were in, we went to consult the urologist. The wait in the doctor's office felt interminable but proved to be worth it when she told us that my growth was benign. My wife burst into tears, and we floated out onto the streets of New York.

This was a "deliverance moment" for us, giving Ps 116 special force:

For you have delivered my soul from death,
my eyes from tears,
my feet from stumbling. (Ps 116:8)

CELEBRATING GOD'S RESCUE

Read the whole psalm aloud.

I love the LORD, because he has heard
my voice and my pleas for mercy.
Because he inclined his ear to me,
therefore I will call on him as long as I live.
The snares of death encompassed me;
the pangs of Sheol laid hold on me;
I suffered distress and anguish.
Then I called on the name of the LORD:
"O LORD, I pray, deliver my soul!"

Gracious is the LORD, and righteous;
our God is merciful.
The LORD preserves the simple;
when I was brought low, he saved me.
Return, O my soul, to your rest;
for the LORD has dealt bountifully with you.

For you have delivered my soul from death,
my eyes from tears,
my feet from stumbling;
I will walk before the LORD
in the land of the living.

I believed, even when I spoke,
"I am greatly afflicted";
I said in my alarm,
"All mankind are liars."

What shall I render to the LORD
for all his benefits to me?
I will lift up the cup of salvation
and call on the name of the LORD,
I will pay my vows to the LORD
in the presence of all his people.

Precious in the sight of the LORD
    is the death of his saints.
O LORD, I am your servant;
    I am your servant, the son of your maidservant.
    You have loosed my bonds.
I will offer to you the sacrifice of thanksgiving
    and call on the name of the LORD.
I will pay my vows to the LORD
    in the presence of all his people,
in the courts of the house of the LORD,
    in your midst, O Jerusalem.
Praise the LORD! (Ps 116:1–19)

Here we have a buoyant song of rescue. God has delivered the psalmist from a terrible affliction (much worse than mine!)—from death, shame, stumbling, tears, and vicious liars. He is filled with joy and cannot help but summon his "soul" (Ps 116:7) to celebrate before one and all ("in the presence of all his people" [Ps 116:18]) the God who has been so kind to him. Reading his words, we join in the song. Our hearts are stirred afresh with love for God as we recall our own stories of deliverance, both small and great.

NO RESCUE FOR JESUS

But there is more to hear. Psalm 116 belongs to the cluster of psalms called the Egyptian Hallel (Pss 113–118), sung at Passover to recall the "passing over" of the angel of death on the eve of Israel's escape from Egypt. In all likelihood, Jesus sang this psalm with his disciples during the Last Supper, probably at the end.[1]

How, we might ask, did Jesus process Ps 116 as he sang it with his friends, knowing what was soon to happen to him—knowing that the "angel of death" was not, in his case, going to pass over? We don't know exactly. But certainly, the irony of the moment would not have been lost on him,

1. See Mark 14:26. "By custom, the first two psalms were sung before the Passover meal, and the remaining four after it" (Kidner, *Psalms 73–150*, 401). William Lane comments on Mark 14:26: "Jesus took the words of [the Hallel psalms] as his own prayer of thanksgiving and praise. He pledged to keep his vows in the presence of all the people (Ps 116:12–19); he called upon the Gentiles to join in the praise of God (Ps 117) . . . When Jesus arose to go to Gethsemane, Ps 118 was upon his lips. It provided an appropriate description of how God would guide his Messiah through distress and suffering to glory." Lane, *Mark*, 509.

especially as events progressed. For only part of the psalm, the dark part, proved true to his experience.

Think about Jesus' experience. "Distress and anguish" (Ps 116:3) fell upon him with such impact that he collapsed, sweating blood and begging repeatedly to have the cup removed from him ("deliver my soul!" [Ps 116:4]). His enemies led him away in "bonds" (Ps 116:16) to be delivered into the hands of "liars" (Ps 116:11) who falsely accused him. Condemned to crucifixion he "stumbled" (Ps 116:8) under the burden of the cross. The "snares of death encompassed [him], the pangs of Sheol laid hold on [him]" (Ps 116:3), threatening to drag him to a terrible death. And God did not act. The joy of rescue, the Passover deliverance, did not come to him.[2]

JOY ON THE FAR SIDE OF DEATH

What do you make of the "failure" of Ps 116 in Jesus' case? What will help you (and deeply encourage you) is understanding it in the light of the meal Jesus shared just before he sang the psalm with his friends. At the Last Supper, Jesus promised a new Passover—a better one. He was to be the Lamb: his death had to come, for it alone could deliver you and me, not from Egypt (or Rome) but from death itself. The deliverance of Ps 116 would not come to him so that it might come forever to us.[3]

What will also help you understand the "failure" of Ps 116 in Jesus' case is the story of Easter morning when, on the far side of death, Jesus tasted the deliverance denied him on Good Friday. That joy, so vivid in the language of the psalm, is not simply in the postponement of death but in its annihilation. Jesus now "walks before the LORD in the land of the living" (Ps 116:9), never to perish again.[4]

And what compounds Jesus' joy is knowing that he has brought us with him. When we imagine Jesus singing, "I will offer to you the sacrifice

2. See Matt 26:36–44 (describing Jesus' collapse and repeated pleas), Luke 22:44 ("his sweat became like great drops of blood"), Luke 23:26 (Simon was compelled to carry the cross because Jesus was too weak), John 18:12 (his captors "bound him"), Mark 14:56 ("many bore false witness against him"), and Luke 23:46 ("he breathed his last").

3. See Luke 22:14–20 and parallels. See also John 14:2 where Jesus speaks of "go[ing] to prepare a place for [us]."

4. "I am the resurrection and the life. Whoever believes in me, though he die, yet shall he live" (John 11:25). On Easter, Jesus walked with his disciples along the Emmaus Road, so filled with that new life that his disciples' hearts "burn[ed] within [them]" (Luke 24:32), as he explained it to them.

of thanksgiving . . . I will pay my vows to the LORD *in the presence of all his people*" (Ps 116:17, 18), we discover that a significant element in his delight is that he will be singing in our company—for he will bring us with him in his triumph.

EASTER'S MEANING FOR JESUS

Read aloud again the following portions of Ps 116, this time imagining Jesus saying them on Easter morning.

> I love the LORD, because he has heard
> my voice and my pleas for mercy . . .
> The snares of death encompassed me;
> the pangs of Sheol laid hold on me;
> I suffered distress and anguish.
> Then I called on the name of the LORD:
> "O LORD, I pray, deliver my soul!"
> Gracious is the LORD, and righteous;
> our God is merciful.
> The LORD preserves the simple;
> when I was brought low, he saved me . . .
> What shall I render to the LORD
> for all his benefits to me?
> I will lift up the cup of salvation
> and call on the name of the LORD,
> I will pay my vows to the LORD
> in the presence of all his people. (Ps 116:1, 3–6, 12–14)

It is easy to reflect on what Easter means for us. But do we think enough of what it meant for Jesus—the one true man who had surrendered all to honor his Father and to rescue us—who had gone to hell and back, bearing our sins and his Father's frown into dark and unimaginable places? And now, his faithful, costly, and solitary work completed, the Father has gathered him back, honoring him with praise and delight.

It takes faith to see the joy of the Son in this great reversal—for his resurrection appearances in the Gospels reveal a quiet majesty rather than the exuberant delight we find in our psalm. But the Bible tells us that "for the joy that was set before him [Jesus] endured the cross, despising the shame."[5] So perhaps Ps 116 exists in part to show something about Jesus' experience

5. Heb 12:2.

that the Gospels do not. Perhaps we should let it do its work. It will be good for us to put our Lord, rather than ourselves, at the center of the story.

DARK CLOUD LIFTING

Think again of Ps 116 as our song. There is a cloud that hovers over it, for it celebrates no more than temporary deliverance from death and distress. For everyone who lives to write such a song, there are scores who do not, and even those who do will eventually pass into the silence of "Sheol" (Ps 116:3). A cynical friend might say that the joy of the psalm actually (if unintentionally) mocks us in the light of what is bound to come: "Kidney cancer may not have done you in, Charlie, but something else will!"

But when we imagine Jesus singing Ps 116 with us on history's last day, the cloud lifts and the mocking goes silent. When, in other words, we behold Jesus' story in these words, and when we trust that we will share his triumph, we begin to grasp that every deliverance we have enjoyed in this life, whether large or small, every new morning after a hard night, has been a promise of something greater. For Jesus has entered our story to carry us through it, through death itself, and to bring us home.

PRECIOUS DEATH

Look again at verse 15: "Precious in the eyes of the LORD is the death of his saints." For the psalmist this likely meant, "My brush with death weighed upon the Lord, as will my actual death when it comes, for those who trust him are dear to him."[6] Our dying carries this meaning as well: God was not indifferent to my cancer scare and its imagined impact on my family.

But when we look for Jesus' story in these words, a greater depth opens to us. Of all the saintly deaths that have ever weighed upon the Father's heart, Jesus' death was the dearest, for it was the offering of a life that had never faltered in its love for God and people. And it was doubly precious, for it was offered in substitution for us, whose deaths also weigh upon God's heart.

Think about it. Jesus' offering, because it was perfect and freely given, makes your death precious in a new sense: "For me to live is Christ," writes

6. "*Precious* could mean either 'highly valued' or, in a less happy sense, 'costly.'" Kidner, *Psalms 73–150*, 410.

Paul, "and to die is gain" (Phil 1:21). Death has become a door for you if you belong to Jesus—the way safely home so that you can "walk before the Lord in the land of the living," both now and forever.

Lord Jesus, you came to us from the Father to make vivid and certain his determination to deliver us from all that is wrong in and around us. By his power and grace you fed the hungry, healed the sick, restored the lonely, gathered friends around your table, and lifted those who were struggling out of moments and seasons of helplessness and danger.

Most consolingly you annihilated the power and fear of death through your own tears and stumbling. Your death has become precious to me, for it guarantees that my last day in this life will not be my last. It promises that every reprieve I have known here has been a prelude to a fullness that I cannot now come close to imagining.

Help me, Lord, to remember your daily kindnesses. But help me not to be so mindful of them that I cling to them too tightly, disdaining what lies ahead. Amen.

16

Vindicated

Psalm 18

He rescued me, because he delighted in me. The LORD dealt with me according to my righteousness, according to the cleanness of my hands he rewarded me.

(Ps 18:19–20)

ONCE WHEN ONE OF my nephews was accused of biting the finger of his little brother, he protested, "But his finger was in my mouth when my teeth were closing." Not my fault! We laugh at such behavior in our children. We grow angry and frustrated when we see it in adults who have been caught in scandal.

But some of David's words in Ps 18 take our breath away:

> [The LORD] rescued me, because he delighted in me.
> The LORD dealt with me according to my righteousness . . .
> For all his rules were before me
> and his statutes I did not put away from me.
> I was blameless before him. (Ps 18:19–20, 22–23)

Not only does David deny that he did something wrong. He denies that he did anything wrong. He asserts a level of innocence that is beyond us: "*All* his rules [not just some of them] were before me . . . I was *blameless* before him." What do you make of this?

Before trying to answer this question, it will help to consider the psalm as a whole. Like numerous other psalms (Pss 22 and 69 come to mind), Ps 18 tells a sweeping story. It carries us from personal misery through personal deliverance to cosmic triumph. It is David's signature song, so rich a documentation of his story and hopes that we find it repeated in 2 Sam 22, immediately before the record of his final words. According to its title, the psalm marks the final consolidation of David's reign following the death of Saul and the subjugation of his enemies inside and outside of Israel.

READING PS 18

Read aloud the following portion of Ps 18, and as you do, ask two questions: (1) Why does David choose to describe his deliverance so cosmically? And (2) What sense are we to make of David's claim of innocence?

> I love you, O LORD, my strength.
> The LORD is my rock and my fortress and my deliverer,
>   my God, my rock, in whom I take refuge,
>   my shield, and the horn of my salvation, my stronghold.
> I call upon the LORD, who is worthy to be praised,
>   and I am saved from my enemies.
>
> The cords of death encompassed me;
>   the torrents of destruction assailed me;
> the cords of Sheol entangled me;
>   the snares of death confronted me.
>
> In my distress I called upon the LORD;
>   to my God I cried for help.
> From his temple he heard my voice,
>   and my cry to him reached his ears.
> Then the earth reeled and rocked;
>   the foundations also of the mountains trembled
>   and quaked, because he was angry.
> Smoke went up from his nostrils,
>   and devouring fire from his mouth;
>   glowing coals flamed forth from him.
> He bowed the heavens and came down;
>   thick darkness was under his feet.

He rode on a cherub and flew;
    he came swiftly on the wings of the wind.
He made darkness his covering, his canopy around him,
    thick clouds dark with water.
Out of the brightness before him
    hailstones and coals of fire broke through his clouds.

The LORD also thundered in the heavens,
    and the Most High uttered his voice,
    hailstones and coals of fire.
And he sent out his arrows and scattered them;
    he flashed forth lightnings and routed them.
Then the channels of the sea were seen,
    and the foundations of the world were laid bare
at your rebuke, O LORD,
    at the blast of the breath of your nostrils.

He sent from on high, he took me;
    he drew me out of many waters.
He rescued me from my strong enemy
    and from those who hated me,
    for they were too mighty for me.
They confronted me in the day of my calamity,
    but the LORD was my support.
He brought me out into a broad place;
    he rescued me, because he delighted in me.

The LORD dealt with me according to my righteousness;
    according to the cleanness of my hands he rewarded me.
For I have kept the ways of the LORD,
    and have not wickedly departed from my God.
For all his rules were before me,
    and his statutes I did not put away from me.
I was blameless before him,
    and I kept myself from my guilt.
So the LORD has rewarded me according to my righteousness,
    according to the cleanness of my hands in his sight.
    (Ps 18:1–24)

COSMIC RESCUE

David, or the psalmist writing in David's name,[1] chooses to describe the consolidation of his reign in terms that Peter Jackson would delight to put on film. In words that are full of allusion to Israel's and the world's larger story (the Egyptian plagues, the crossing of the Red Sea, the terrifying earth tremors at Mt. Sinai, perhaps even the creation of the world), we meet the Lord, gathered into his cosmic chariot and riding down the heavens on the wings of a mighty storm. Hail descends, darkness falls, the earth shakes, and lightning lays bare the channels of the sea as the Lord, full of love and vindicating fury for David, lifts him from the raging waters and brings him to safety.

We can perhaps begin to understand the colorful language when we think about the intensity and longevity of David's struggles. Anointed many years before by Samuel, he had never experienced the privileges of kingship. A fugitive, he had lived in wilderness caves and even among the Philistines, where he stayed alive by feigning madness. He had been forced to separate from his dearest friend Jonathan and had seen faithful friends murdered because of their association with him. His life had been lonely and desperate for a long time, existing on very little but the hope that his anointing at Samuel's hand meant something. For these reasons, his vindication, though it was not literally cosmic, had to *feel* cosmic, and therefore he reached deeply into his religious tradition to find words to describe it.[2]

CELEBRATING OUR BIG STORIES

We do something similar when we experience a great deliverance, reaching for dramatic words and songs to communicate our inward delight and relief. When the prisoners in the Rokuroshi POW camp learned from a US torpedo bomber overhead that Japan had surrendered and that they were free from their torment, they were beside themselves with joy:

> In seconds, masses of naked men were stampeding out of the river and up the hill. As the plane turned loops above, the pilot waving, the POWs swarmed into the compound, out of their minds with

1. Scholars debate the meaning of the psalms' titles. Even those with a high view of biblical inspiration note that the titles are not themselves necessarily part of the canon. You can read Kidner, *Psalms 1–72*, 32–36, and Longman, *Psalms*, 40–42, for helpful (and brief) discussions of the issue.

2. First Samuel 16—Second Samuel 6 tells the long and painful story of David's ascent to the throne—as many as 15 years.

> relief and rapture. Their fear of the guards, of the massacre they had so long awaited, was gone, dispersed by the roar and the muscle of the bomber. The prisoners jumped up and down, shouted, and sobbed. Some scrambled onto the camp roofs, waving their arms and singing out their joy to the pilot above. Others piled against the camp fence and sent it crashing over. Someone found matches, and soon, the entire length of the fence was burning.[3]

Any poet who had been at Rokuroshi that day would have used hyperbolic language to describe what happened.

THE DEEPER STORY

But there is more than hyperbole going on in Ps 18. For David knew that his story was not his alone. God had anointed him king of Abraham's people—the people by whom God intended to overcome the darkness into which the world had fallen. He knew that a thousand years before him, God had promised Abraham, "I will make of you a great nation . . . In you all the families of the earth shall be blessed."[4]

David chose cosmic language to describe his rescue because he believed that the story into which God had woven his life was this greater story. He did not know precisely how God was going to bless the families of the earth through his people. He did not know what we know—that his story of waiting, suffering, rescue, and vindication foreshadowed the story of Jesus. But he did know that God was up to something great in him. This is why the whole world and eternity are on his mind as the psalm ends:

> For this I will praise you, O LORD, *among the nations,*
> and sing to your name.
> Great salvation he brings to his king,
> and shows steadfast love to his anointed,
> to David and his offspring *forever.* (Ps 18:49–50)

BREATH-TAKING INNOCENCE

There is a second shocking feature in Ps 18. You will find it in what I have already noted about David's wild explanation for why God rescued him.

3. Hillenbrand, *Unbroken*, 306.

4. Gen 12:2, 3.

The LORD dealt with me according to my righteousness;
according to the cleanness of my hands he rewarded me.
For I have kept the ways of the LORD,
and have not wickedly departed from my God.
For all his rules were before me,
and his statutes I did not put away from me.
I was blameless before him,
and I kept myself from my guilt.
So the LORD has rewarded me according to my righteousness,
according to the cleanness of my hands in his sight.
(Ps 18:20–24)

David is saying, repeatedly(!), "What motivated God to move heaven and earth for my rescue was not his mercy: it was my righteousness." These words confuse us, arising as they do from the songs that so often admit to great moral failure. Psalms 130 and 51 come to mind:

If you, O LORD, should mark iniquities,
O Lord, who could stand? (Ps 130:3)

Have mercy on me, O God,
according to your steadfast love;
according to your abundant mercy
blot out my transgressions. (Ps 51:1)

Ask yourself, how could David have ever written Ps 18:20–24? Can you hear yourself saying what he says? Hasn't God told you and me that we are "by grace . . . saved through faith. And this is not [our] own doing . . . *so that no one may boast*"? (Eph 2:8, 9).

RELATIVE INNOCENCE?

David's assertions of innocence must, we tell ourselves, predate those of the man who would one day rape Bathsheba and then see to her husband Uriah's death.[5] We can forgive them perhaps as the expression of youthful exuberance and moral naivety.

And we can even perhaps receive these words as relatively true, provided we lower the bar on the meaning of moral purity that Jesus confronts us with in the Sermon on the Mount. David may not have been perfect, but

5. Second Samuel 11 tells the story.

he had refused multiple times to take his kingship by force, waiting instead on God's timing.[6]

Reading David's assertions this way helps us understand, at least in part, how to make them our own. We certainly are not perfect, we say, but when we are falsely accused of a particular crime, either as children or defendants in a court case, and are then acquitted, we may properly thank God with David for dealing with us "according to [our] righteousness" in the matter at hand.

Nevertheless, the language of innocence does not quite fit. It is too extreme: "For all his rules were before me, and his statutes I did not put away from me" (Ps 18:22). *All* his rules—really? We may be innocent of the "matter at hand," but what about other matters? What about our motives? If we are honest, the hope of a just vindication, certainly from the hands of a God who sees everything, fades. David's words may even make us feel guilty because they sound too much like our tendency to hide from our guilty selves with bluster.

THE COSMIC VINDICATION OF JESUS

Try a thought experiment. Imagine Jesus singing David's words of cosmic vindication on Easter morning. If you do, the difficult features in those words will disappear. Better, they will cease to be difficulties altogether. They will rather burst with bright meaning. For Jesus' resurrection was in fact a cosmic, world-changing event. God drew his beloved and perfectly obedient Son out of death, setting in motion the end of death for us all. And the rescue in this case was completely deserved. It was not a mighty act of divine mercy but a mighty act of divine justice. Jesus did not stay dead because he had never deserved to die.

Jesus' vindication on Easter was muted to human eyes and ears. No one saw the actual moment of resurrection. Those who met the risen Lord were relatively few and were not rocked by heavenly choirs and lights. But Ps 18 helps us see what was actually happening in the Real World—the world that counts—the world we as yet only see by faith. The heavenly Father came racing down the heavens in the early hours of that great day, filled with the passion of vindicating love for the Son in whom he delights and who had unjustly endured outrageous treatment at our hands. And

6. See 1 Sam 24 and 26.

as the Father took Jesus in his arms, heaven itself erupted in loud songs of praise over the victory of the Beloved.

VINDICATED IN JESUS

I trust you can see from what I have just said that Easter isn't *about* you (or me) first and foremost. It is about the Son and his Father overthrowing the dark and deadly rebellion of this world. But Easter does *involve* you, if you belong by faith to God's beloved Son. God "delight[s] in [you]" (Ps 18:19) and for that reason will vindicate you. He will do this not because you are, as yet, all that God means for you to be—but because you are one with your elder brother who willingly made himself one with you and God delights in him.

"Yet once more I will shake not only the earth but also the heavens" (Heb 12:26), cries the Lord. One day, soon perhaps, God will ride down the heavens like the torpedo bomber descending upon the POWs at Rokuroshi. He will come without reluctance or the mutedness of Easter morning but with burning justice bent upon our vindication, for we are his holy ones, innocent in Jesus. It would be a terrible—and impossible—denial of his character not to. And it would be a tragedy beyond calculation for you or me not to be found in Jesus on that day.

Jesus, my Brother and my King, I delight with you at your cosmic vindication on Easter morning. I rejoice with the joy of the Father as I picture him riding down the heavens to pull you from death and shame, declaring that death had no claim over you and naming you the Lord of all. I join the heavenly choir and anticipate the whole cosmos rising to declare with delight that you alone among the human race are truly good, the one and only human being fully worthy to be called the Image of God.

Why, Lord Jesus, you chose to identify so fully with me—why you chose to make your moral beauty my own—I will never fully understand. I can only thank you that you have. I can only thank you that now and forever your justice is fully on my side. By the might of your Spirit, make me more and more like you, more fully human, as I wait for the day when you finish your work in me. Don't let me ever take lightly who I am in you and what it cost you to make this so. Amen.

17

Cursing: Hating Evil

Psalm 69

Let them be blotted out of the book of the living; let them not be enrolled among the righteous.

(Ps 69:28)

Read aloud the following section from Ps 69:

Let their own table before them become a snare;
    and when they are at peace, let it become a trap.
Let their eyes be darkened, so that they cannot see,
    and make their loins tremble continually.
Pour out your indignation upon them,
    and let your burning anger overtake them.
May their camp be a desolation;
    let no one dwell in their tents . . .
Add to them punishment upon punishment;
    may they have no acquittal from you.
Let them be blotted out of the book of the living;
    let them not be enrolled among the righteous.
    (Ps 69:22–25, 27–28)

RUIN AND MORE

Think for a moment of the frightful things David is saying.

- First, he wants the good things that God has given his enemies to imprison them:

  Let their own table before them become a snare;
  and when they are at peace, let it become a trap. (Ps 69:22)

  In modern terms, he is praying for food and alcohol addictions. He is praying that their vacation home in the Poconos or Lake Tahoe will become a financial drain. He is praying that their retirement funds will be depleted, making them destitute. He is praying that their friends will manipulate and control them.

- Second, he wants them blindly anxious:

  Let their eyes be darkened, so that they cannot see,
  and make their loins tremble continually. (Ps 69:23)

  "Make them worry all the time," David cries, "but keep them from seeing why. Confuse them. Fill them with panic."

- Third, David wants them socially ruined:

  May their camp be a desolation;
  let no one dwell in their tents. (Ps 69:25)

  Picture New York, or your hometown, void of human habitation, a ghost town with nothing there but wild animals. Worse, imagine that nothing lives there at all—just heaps of trash dwarfing the sky.

Ruin—desolation—loneliness—defeat. But that's not all. David calls down God's fury on his foes:

> *Pour out* your indignation upon them,
> and let your *burning anger* overtake them . . .
> Add to them *punishment upon punishment*;
> may they have *no acquittal* from you.
> Let them be *blotted out* of the book of the living;
> let them not be enrolled among the righteous.
> (Ps 69:24, 27–28)

David wants his enemies overwhelmed by God's wrath, with no hope of reprieve. He wants them excluded forever from life, shut out from God and his people, lost in what Jesus would later call "outer darkness."[1] C. S. Lewis invites us to catch a glimpse of this condition when he pictures Napoleon alone in his mansion, a vast distance from the center of hell, endlessly pacing as he endlessly relives the Battle of Waterloo.[2]

This is pretty fierce stuff. Derek Kidner summarizes well what David wants his enemies to lose:

> [The curse] enumerates . . . the things that normally make life worth living: at one level, food and fellowship; one's faculties and strength ("eyes . . . loins"); a place to belong to; and more fundamentally, the goodwill of God . . . His clearance from guilt (27 sic), and to be known and accepted by Him (28 sic).[3]

JESUS' VOICE?

I imagine that these words disturb you, especially in the light of what we have been saying about listening for Jesus' voice in the psalms. For didn't Jesus say, "Love your enemies, do good to those who hate you, bless those who curse you, pray for those who abuse you"? (Luke 6:27–28).

There seems to be a flat-out contradiction here. What do we do with it? Do we remind ourselves that the psalms (like the rest of the Scriptures) have dual authorship—both human and divine (which is true)—and then with relief say that verses 22–28 are only David's words and that other parts of the psalm (say, verse 9, "Zeal for your house has consumed me") are the Messiah's? Do we say that this section of the psalm (like other, similar sections in other psalms) is not "as inspired" as some others (whatever that means)? Or do we just skip this part? Do we draw a big red "x" right though verses 22–28?

I think that such solutions are too easy, given Jesus' claim that "the Law of Moses and the Prophets and the Psalms" culminate in him.[4] We must find a way for these tough words to "make [us] wise for salvation through faith in Christ Jesus."[5] We must find a way to allow them somehow to reflect Jesus' voice and mind.

1. See Matt 22:13.
2. See Lewis, *Divorce*, 20–21.
3. Kidner, *Psalm 1–72*, 248.
4. Luke 24:44. See also John 5:39 ("the Scriptures bear witness about me").
5. 2 Tim 3:15.

To find our way I will ask two questions, the first in this chapter and the second in the next: (1) What's right with these words, and (2) What's missing?

JUSTICE IN THE COSMOS

Here is one of the things that is right about these difficult words. They assume that we live in a world that is governed by a just God who will one day put everything right. One of the Batman films is particularly dark, largely because of the character of the Joker, who destroys for the sake of destroying. Hitler's cruelty was driven by a vision, however corrupted, for the good of the German people. But the Joker has no vision whatsoever, not even one that he sees as positive. The idea of a morally ordered cosmos is nonsense to him.

For David the world can be terrible, but it is not a joke. Wrong is wrong—and it must be punished. There is a God who can and must make things right.

David reflects the mind of Jesus. When Jesus says, "Judge not, that you be not judged," he does not mean that there are no judgments to be made. For he goes on to say, "First, take the log out of your own eye, and then you will see clearly to take the speck out of your brother's" (Matt 7:1, 5). Jesus' prohibition is not against making judgments but against arrogantly doing so. He himself will "strike down the nations."[6]

When Jesus cried out,

> Woe to you, scribes and Pharisees . . . blind guides, straining at a gnat and swallowing a camel . . . full of greed and self-indulgence . . . whitewashed tombs . . . full of dead people's bones . . . full of hypocrisy and lawlessness . . . Fill up, then, the measure of your fathers. You serpents, you brood of vipers, how are you to escape being sentenced to hell,"[7]

he was not at odds with his own teaching. He was acting upon the reality that there is justice in the cosmos, and it is right to pronounce in its favor.

6. Rev 19:15.

7. Matt 23:23, 24, 25, 27, 28, 32–33.

A WORLD WITHOUT JUSTICE?

Imagine a world where the Joker's vision of things (an amoral chaos) is in fact true. We could not stand such a world—and it is self-evidently not the world in which we live, both by intuition and practice. We hold our children accountable because we believe there exist standards to which they ought to be accountable. We have legislators who seek to give shape to how we should order our life together and courts that seek to enforce that order (albeit imperfectly), because justice is real.

Shortly after 9/11, my wife and I were pulled over and ticketed wrongly by a police officer who treated us so harshly that we were terrified. We were also incensed. Everything in us screamed, "This is wrong! It must be righted. This man should be reprimanded." That sense of outrage in us is what lies at the root of David's outburst in Ps 69 and reflects the same sort of outrage that we find in Jesus' denunciation of the Pharisees.

Here is the point. The problem we have with judgment, if we really think about it, is not judgment per se. It is the sort of judgment Jeannie and I experienced—abusive judgment, unfair judgment. David is onto something right when he calls upon God to judge those "who hate me without cause" (Ps 69:4).

PUTTING JUDGMENT INTO THE HANDS OF GOD

One of the things we often miss about the cursing in the psalms is that it does not issue in actual violence. The curses are delivered upwards to God and left in his hands (this is a second thing that Ps 69 gets right). When the psalmist cries, "Pour out your indignation upon them, and let your burning anger overtake them" (Ps 69:24), he is relinquishing to God the task of executing judgment. Paul tells us to do the same thing:

> Beloved, never avenge yourselves, but leave it to the wrath of God, for it is written, "Vengeance is mine, I will repay, says the Lord." (Rom 12:19)

When our friends speak of preferring the "New Testament God of love" to the "Old Testament God of wrath," they reveal that they have not read their New Testaments very well. They correctly see an extraordinary emphasis on mercy in the New Testament, but they miss the moral backdrop out of which that mercy appears. Justice does not disappear with the arrival of Jesus. It is rather resoundingly vindicated by Jesus, who surrenders his cause to God, just as David did, and then proceeds to satisfy justice by bearing its sanctions himself as our substitute.

PASSION FOR GOD

A third thing that's right about David's words is that they are not just about him. David understands himself to be God's anointed king—positioned by God to represent him in a world that his grown hostile to him. You may recall the esteem that David attached to that office even before he occupied it. More than once mad king Saul, bent on destroying David, falls into the fugitive's hands. But David refuses to touch him or even permit one of his soldiers to do so:

> As the LORD lives, the LORD will strike him, or his day will come to die, or he will go down into battle and perish. The LORD forbid that I should put out my hand against the LORD's anointed. (1 Sam 26:10–11)

When the "Lord's anointed" (whether David or Saul) is attacked, the LORD himself is attacked. This both restrains David (because Saul is God's anointed) and infuriates David (because he, too, is God's anointed). David's rage arises, at least in part, from the same source as Jesus' rage over the money changers in the temple: horror at the abuse of God's name.

HATING EVIL WITH JESUS

What does this mean for us as we try to meet Jesus in these difficult words of David? It means that, though we may not hate our enemies (Jesus forbids this—he alone is the judge), we may hate evil. We may, in fact must, get worked up about the abuse of God's reputation, of God's law, and of God's image-bearers (that is, people). If we paraphrase and augment verses 24–28 a bit, we can find a way to echo the words of the heavenly Judge without presuming to be that Judge ourselves:

> Pour out your indignation upon [idolatry and injustice],
> and let your burning anger overtake [these habits of the human
> heart in me and in the hearts of my colleagues,
> children and friends] . . .
> Add to them punishment upon punishment;
> may they have no acquittal from you [May sin find no

acquittal, may excuses for sin and blame-shifting end].
Let [sin] be blotted out [May false worship and cruelty be
annihilated from every human heart and deed] . . .
let [such falsehood] not be enrolled among the righteous
[May it have nothing to do with us]. (Ps 69:24, 27–28)

We are so often guilt-ridden by our own misplaced anger, by hatred that we know is wrongly directed. How refreshing to know that there are things (behaviors and attitudes) that we are permitted, and even commanded, to hate and that we are not at odds with Jesus when we do. In fact, to put the matter more strongly, we find ourselves giving voice to Jesus' own fury against sin and evil when we do. What is more, we find ourselves beginning to understand why Jesus was so livid with Peter ("Get behind me, Satan!" [Matt 16:23]) when the disciple rebuked him for his determination to suffer and die in Jerusalem. For by that very suffering Jesus intended to bring his wrath down upon sin and its effects, and any suggestion that he not do so was intolerable to him.

So, get angry with evil. Hate it with fully engaged fury. Jesus does, and you can too.

Lord Jesus Christ, seated in glory at your Father's right hand, you are full of goodness and grace, but this does not make you soft when it comes to sin and evil. Precisely because you are good, you hate with a perfect, ever-present and never-ending fullness all that is wrong in us and in our world. When you came among us as one of us, you did so to annihilate evil. Your every word, deed, and gesture, culminating in the great conflict at the cross, was an assault upon human lying, idolatry, cruelty, and indifference. You bore my sins because you hated them and intended to tear them forever from my life.

Help me, great Redeemer, to hate what you hate. Help me to do this by the power of your Holy Spirit under the protection of your cross. Amen.

18

Cursing and the Cross

Psalm 69

I have great sorrow and unceasing anguish in my heart. For I could wish that I myself were accursed and cut off from Christ for the sake of my brothers, my kinsmen according to the flesh.

(Rom 9:2–3)

Read again the following portion of Ps 69, imagining Jesus processing it with you. What might Jesus say is missing from these words?

> Let their own table before them become a snare;
> and when they are at peace, let it become a trap.
> Let their eyes be darkened, so that they cannot see,
> and make their loins tremble continually.
> Pour out your indignation upon them,
> and let your burning anger overtake them.
> May their camp be a desolation;
> let no one dwell in their tents.
> For they persecute him whom you have struck down,
> and they recount the pain of those you have wounded.
> Add to them punishment upon punishment;
> may they have no acquittal from you.
> Let them be blotted out of the book of the living;
> let them not be enrolled among the righteous. (Ps 69:22–28)

What is missing from these words are patience and compassion, and this is understandable because these qualities arise from Jesus' death and resurrection, both of which were a thousand years into the future when David wrote.

PATIENCE RISING

Think first of patience. Knowing what we know, now that Christ has come, can make us more patient than David was able to be because it opens to our eyes the guarantee that all will be put right by God. David had a pressing need for vindication because his picture of life beyond the horizons of the life he knew was fuzzy. For all he knew, if he (and therefore the God he represented) were not exonerated and vindicated here and now, they might never be.

But the cross, and what followed, changes all this. Jesus bore horrible abuse in silence—without retaliation—in part because he foresaw the resurrection. He knew that his Father would sort things out—that justice would be done. And God did (and will) sort things out, raising Jesus from the dead and honoring him with all authority and the right to "judge the living and the dead," as we have grown accustomed to say in the Nicene Creed.

Think of how Jesus' death and resurrection can make you patient. Because God has vindicated Jesus and has appointed him to put everything right when all is said and done, you don't have to scream at the woman who honks at you repeatedly when you are lost in traffic. You don't have to demand an absolutely fair grade, or the immediate end of racism, or perfect equity in the government's distribution of tax revenues, or in your boss's hiring, promotion, and firing practices. You don't have to explain yourself to your angry neighbor until you are fully understood and your rights and innocence are fully acknowledged. Jesus will perfectly sort it all out in due time. Justice is coming!

GOD MUST SORT THINGS OUT

And Jesus *must* sort things out. The problem with you or me demanding full and immediate justice now is that things at present are always more complicated than we think. People everywhere are caught between heaven and hell—no one is as confirmed in nihilistic evil as is the Joker. Every enemy is a potential friend. Many who cried out for Jesus' death repented only weeks later on Pentecost and its aftermath.[1]

One day you and I may find ourselves saying with Jesus, "Let them be blotted out of the book of the living" (Ps 69:28). But that will happen only when the enemies of God are so fully confirmed in their hatred of God that they themselves want nothing but to be removed forever from God's presence (which is what being "blotted out" amounts to when you think about it).

Those terrible words of judgment will, in other words, be said (the difficult parts of Ps 69 turn out in fact to have been inspired after all!). But they will not force people to go to a place they do not seek. Rather those words will confirm people in their determination to be done with God. Now, today, such words are premature. We must wait for Jesus to sort through the hearts of people. And the cross and resurrection guarantee that he will.

COMPASSION RISING

The cross does a second thing to the curses of Ps 69. It transforms their tone dramatically: vengefulness gives way to compassion. Why? Because Jesus' death reveals a God who willingly took those curses upon himself so that people like you and me could escape them.

Tweak verses 22–23 and 28 so that they describe what Jesus endured, and you will see what I mean:

> Let [Jesus'] own table . . . become a snare. (Ps 69:22)
>
> > The Passover meal—and the fellowship of the disciples—became the fellowship from which Jesus' betrayer, denier, and deserters arose.
>
> Let [Jesus'] eyes be darkened, so that [he] cannot see,
> and make [his] loins tremble continually. (Ps 69:23)
>
> > Jesus, who had no cause to collapse under the judgment of God, fell to the ground in the Garden of Gethsemane—unable to stand because of the unbearable dread of what was coming. And then, at the cross, he "lost sight" of his Father (his eyes were "darkened") as judgment fell upon him and the Father withdrew.

1. See Acts 2:37, 47, and Acts 6:7.

> Let [Jesus] be blotted out of the book of the living;
> let [him] not be enrolled among the righteous. (Ps 69:28)

Jesus died—and he died alone—an outcast—excluded from Israel.

FIRESTORM OF CURSING

Something even more frightful also happened. We are told that as Jesus hung panting, slowly dying of thirst and asphyxiation, a terrible darkness rose upon the land, and a terrible cry ("Why have you forsaken me!") burst from Jesus' lips. That rising darkness accompanied and depicted the heaping up of "punishment upon punishment" (yours and mine [Ps 69:27]) upon the shoulders of Jesus, crushing him. And that cry arose from profound desolation as wave upon wave of God's "indignation" and "burning anger" overtook him (Ps 69:24).

Not a spark but a firestorm of cursing, not a trickle but a deluge—far greater than David was ever able to call down upon his enemies—came down upon God's Son as he died. All the fury of God against the heaped-up insults and injustices of this world (can we really count them?) fell upon Jesus until the indignation of the perfect Judge, who sees all, remembers all (how easily we forget) and must punish all, burned out. Jesus became a burnt offering, "consumed" by "zeal" (Ps 69:9) for his Father's honor and love for people like you and me.

This suffering gave no pleasure to the Father; it broke his heart to bring Jesus under this deluge of cursing. Nor did Jesus endure it involuntarily, as if the Father had forced it upon him. Father and Son, together, chose terrible, unmeasurable suffering because love for us necessitated it.

WHY THE FIRESTORM?

I have had difficulty understanding this necessity. I suspect that you have as well. Here is something of how I have tried to explain it to myself.

We can know the suffering of God was necessary not because we can understand it. We know it was necessary simply because it happened—because God, who sees with much greater moral clarity than we do and who cares far more deeply than we do about what is right and true, brought it to pass. Would God, we should ask ourselves, have endured Good Friday if he had at his disposal another way to put things right with us?

Rather than seek fully to make sense of the firestorm that fell on Jesus, we would do better to seek to learn from it. Thomas Kelly, an Irish churchman writing over two hundred years ago, helps us:

> Ye who think of sin but lightly nor suppose the evil great
> Here may view its nature rightly, here its guilt may estimate.
> Mark the sacrifice appointed, see who bears the awful load;
> 'Tis the Word, the Lord's anointed, Son of Man and Son of God.[2]

If God himself had to endure the punishment for our sin, and if that punishment was for him so overwhelming, then our sin must be God-sized and far more odious than we are capable of calculating.

HUMBLED HEARTS

Think of how discovering and reflecting on the necessity of God's freely chosen suffering can change us—we who otherwise might be tempted to blow up at people who offend us. It can make us less apt to blame them, even when they are wrong. How can we fly to judgment when we deserve judgment ourselves (our crimes may be different, and perhaps more subtle, but they are still sins—and deeply offensive to God) and when we know that God himself has borne ours?

With this insight, our tone toward those who hurt us begins to shift. Our assessment that they have done wrong may persist (they may well have done wrong), although it no longer rings with vindictiveness—but with sadness.

This very shift happens with Paul, whose heart breaks as he anticipates the curses of verses 22–23 (which he quotes in Rom 11:9–10) falling upon his fellow Jews, many of whom hated him passionately because of his love for Christ:

> I have great sorrow and unceasing anguish in my heart. For I could wish that I myself were accursed and cut off from Christ for the sake of my brothers, my kinsmen according to the flesh. (Rom 9:2–3)

This is what the cross does to the hard words of Ps 69 because it is what it does to us when, like Paul, we understand the cross's meaning for us.

2. Kelly, "Stricken," 257.

SEEING THROUGH THE LENS OF THE CROSS

How do you and I read the curses of Ps 69 (and elsewhere in the psalms) so that they "make [us] wise for salvation through faith in Christ"?[3] How do we hear Jesus' voice, or at least see Jesus' heart, in the troubling words we find there? What I have been saying is that we read them, we see them, through the lens of the cross.

From that vantage point, we discover that Jesus does not, when he speaks so strongly of forgiveness, suddenly introduce us to a world that is fundamentally different from the world of the psalmist—a world in which judgment does not exist, a world in which justice no longer must be satisfied. Rather, he introduces us (better, he reveals to us in final fullness) the God who has always been just—a God who has gone to unimaginable lengths to satisfy justice but in such a way that he has not, and will not, destroy the people he loves—people like you and me. Jesus tells us not to curse our enemies, not because there are no curses to be uttered but because he chose to lay those curses on himself.

CURSES BORNE—ONE WAY OR THE OTHER

I need to end with a word of warning. The curses of Ps 69 must be borne—if not by the Messiah, then by you and me. In some form we all bear them now—in loneliness and alienation, in moments of emptiness, in depression, in debilitating worry, in guilt, in the circumstances of war and oppression, in the outcomes of deceit. If you or I have come under Jesus' cross and protection, these experiences are real, but they are fading—they are vestiges of our former life's sad consequences. But if you or I have not yet chosen to come under Jesus' protection, and if we persist in that choice, then the curses are guarantees of worse things to come.

We don't have to believe that God relishes the prospect of his judgment falling on his creatures (he doesn't) before we can believe that it may happen to us. God takes no "pleasure in the death of the wicked . . . [but] rather that he should turn from his way and live" (Ezek 18:23). James tells us that God's anger is not like ours:[4] ours is always flawed in some way, but God's never is. Nevertheless, judgment, albeit with tears, must come.

3. 2 Tim 3:15.

4. See Jas 1:20.

May we all, and may all those we know and love, be able to sing with John Newton:

> 'Twas grace that taught my heart to fear,
> And grace my fear relieved;
> How precious did that grace appear
> The hour I first believed![5]

Lord Jesus Christ, you are fully human, fully able to identify with me and to help me as I make my way through life in this broken world. But you are also fully God, and in that respect, you are not like me. You are the Creator, I am your creature; you have life in yourself, I live only by your power; you are infinite, I am finite; you are good, I fall short; you are faithful, I break my promises; you love people, I have used them; you see into the depths of the heart, I see only what is on the surface. You have every right to assess me—every right to condemn me. And yet, you have chosen to bear that condemnation yourself.

Forgive me for telling you how to run things, for judging you over things I do not understand, for living as if I were entitled to the good life. Forgive me for taking judgment into my own hands, as if I had the knowledge and the goodness to do it rightly. Forgive me for my blame-shifting and my chosen blindness to my own sin. Above all, forgive me for the folly of my indifference to the price you paid to bring me fully and forever out of the condemnation I deserve. By your Spirit show me, and teach me to love, what is real. Amen.

5. Newton, "Amazing Grace," 460.

19

Sorting Through the Voices

Psalm 118

The stone that the builders rejected has become the cornerstone.
This is the LORD's doing; it is marvelous in our eyes.

(Ps 118:22–23)

MEETING JESUS IN THE psalms may not always be our first instinct. And when we give ourselves to that task, we can discover that it isn't easy. For these reasons I will devote the next three chapters to helping you develop some skills for doing so, starting with sorting through the many voices in the psalms.

One of the fascinating and at times confusing elements of the psalms is their voicing. The speaker and the audience often shift about without warning or annotation. One moment "I" am singing, the next moment "we" are; then, suddenly, another voice (a leader, or a teacher, or God) joins in. Sometimes the psalmist speaks to himself, sometimes to God, and sometimes to other people.

If you listen carefully, you will hear at least three different voices in Ps 118. Sorting them out, which I aim to do in this chapter, won't give you a simple formula for doing so in other psalms. But it will help you to be more alert to the task and encourage you to work at it by opening to you a richness of meaning you might otherwise miss.

As I help you listen for different speakers, I will try especially to distinguish the voice of Jesus in the midst of them all. It will be important to do this, not because I want to deny that Jesus and his story echo throughout the voices we encounter but because there are moments in this psalm when he speaks with such vivid directness that he can get hold of our hearts and imaginations with particular power. We don't want to miss those moments in any psalm.

PS 118

Psalm 118 is one of a cluster of songs that Israelites sang at Passover, commemorating the deliverance from Egypt. Jesus very likely sang it with his disciples following the Last Supper.[1] The psalm speaks to us in at least three voices: the worship leader (or leaders), the congregation, and the witness (like someone giving a personal testimony in a worship service). One wonders if Jesus and his disciples rendered it this way, with different ones among them taking on the different roles. Maybe they did. Here it is with the parts broken out in one possible arrangement.

CALL AND RESPONSE

The worship leader(s)	Oh give thanks to the LORD, for he is good;
(to the congregation)	for his steadfast love endures forever!
	Let Israel say,
	"His steadfast love endures forever."
	Let the house of Aaron say,
	"His steadfast love endures forever."
	Let those who fear the LORD say,
	"His steadfast love endures forever."

1. See Matt 26:30.

The witness (to the congregation)	Out of my distress I called on the LORD; the LORD answered me and set me free. The LORD is on my side; I will not fear. What can man do to me? The LORD is on my side as my helper; I shall look in triumph on those who hate me.
The congregation responding	It is better to take refuge in the LORD than to trust in man. It is better to take refuge in the LORD than to trust in princes.
The witness (to the congregation)	All nations surrounded me; in the name of the LORD I cut them off! They surrounded me, surrounded me on every side; in the name of the LORD I cut them off! They surrounded me like bees; they went out like a fire among thorns; in the name of the LORD I cut them off! I was pushed hard, so that I was falling, but the LORD helped me. The LORD is my strength and my song; he has become my salvation.
The congregation responding	Glad songs of salvation are in the tents of the righteous: "The right hand of the LORD does valiantly, the right hand of the LORD exalts, the right hand of the LORD does valiantly!"

The witness	I shall not die, but I shall live,
(to the congregation)	and recount the deeds of the LORD.
	The LORD has disciplined me severely,
	but he has not given me over to death.
	Open to me the gates of righteousness,
	that I may enter through them
	and give thanks to the LORD.
	This is the gate of the LORD;
	the righteous shall enter through it.
(to God)	I thank you that you have answered me
	and have become my salvation.
The congregation	The stone that the builders rejected
(to one another)	has become the cornerstone.
	This is the LORD's doing;
	it is marvelous in our eyes.
	This is the day that the LORD has made;
	let us rejoice and be glad in it.
(to God)	Save us, we pray, O LORD!
	O LORD, we pray, give us success!
(to one another)	Blessed is he who comes in the name of the LORD!
(to the witness)	We bless you from the house of the LORD.
(to one another)	The LORD is God,
	and he has made his light to shine upon us.
	Bind the festal sacrifice with cords,
	up to the horns of the altar!
The witness	You are my God, and I will give thanks to you;
(to the Lord)	you are my God; I will extol you.
The worship leader(s)	Oh give thanks to the LORD, for he is good;
(to the congregation)	for his steadfast love endures forever!
	(Ps 118:1–29)

MORE VOICES STILL

Overlay the different liturgical voices you have just heard with the voices I have been urging you to listen for in this book, and the reading of this psalm becomes richer still. We can hear four additional voices.

First, we hear the historical voices—the voices of Jesus' disciples and many Jews before them as they declared their faith on the eve of the Passover. They would have done this with a deep sense of their own nation's story, as generations before them had done, recalling in song the great deliverance from Egypt (Would they have identified Moses as the stone "rejected" by Pharaoh whom God had made the "chief cornerstone" when he smote the Egyptians and led his people to freedom?).

We can hear the disciples looking forward as well, recalling with the prophets that the exodus had set in motion the hopes of an even greater deliverance for which they were still waiting. They had exuberantly called out for that deliverance less than a week earlier (remember them joining the children with their "Hosannahs" ("Save us . . . Lord" [Ps 118:25]) as Jesus entered Jerusalem).

But Ps 118 isn't just their song back then. Parts of it at least can be heard as the song of every believer across time (the second voice), recalling great distress at the hands of enemies and the kindness of the Lord in delivering them. You will perhaps hear your own stories of suffering and vindication, stories that have led you to cry jubilantly to your friends:

> Out of my distress I called on the LORD;
> the LORD answered me and set me free . . .
> The LORD is my strength and my song;
> he has become my salvation. (Ps 118:5, 14)

THE DEEP SONG

There is yet a third voice, the one I have been urging you to listen for throughout this book. Peter quotes verse 22 with reference to Jesus:

> You yourselves like living stones are being built up as a spiritual house . . . to offer spiritual sacrifices acceptable to God through Jesus Christ . . . So the honor is for you who believe, but for those who do not believe,

> *"The stone that the builders rejected*
> *has become the cornerstone."*[2]

With Peter's encouragement the "witness" of Ps 118 becomes Jesus and the entire psalm resonates with the sufferings of Good Friday and the great vindication on Easter. We hear Jesus himself giving testimony on Resurrection Day:

> Out of my distress I called on the LORD;
> the LORD answered me and set me free.
> The LORD is on my side; I will not fear.
> What can man do to me? . . .
> They surrounded me like bees;
> they went out like a fire among thorns;
> in the name of the LORD I cut them off!
> I was pushed hard, so that I was falling,
> but the LORD helped me.
> The LORD is my strength and my song;
> he has become my salvation . . .
> You are my God, and I will give thanks to you;
> you are my God; I will extol you. (Ps 118:5–6, 12–14, 28)

Once we hear Jesus speaking, we cannot help hearing verses 1 and 29 as a summons, not just from an earthly worship leader but from heaven itself. That summons comes to us today and across time (from Moses, from Peter, and beyond) to celebrate God's "steadfast love" (Ps 118:29), which we now know beyond doubt "endures forever" (Ps 118:29) and includes us. And this is when we hear our own corporate voice (the fourth one) rising in celebration of God's grace and power, giving Jesus his due:

> Lord Jesus, you are *the stone that the builders rejected*, humiliated and crucified. And now you are triumphant, the *cornerstone* of a whole new people and world. What a wonder you are, O Lord. What you have done is *marvelous in our eyes. This . . . day*, the day of resurrection, everything has become new. We will *rejoice and be glad in it.* How *good* you are, how *steadfast* your *love* is, *enduring forever.*

2. 1 Pet 2:5, 7.

ONE SONG

Back in the Introduction, I mentioned the "Ode to Joy" in the last movement of Beethoven's *Ninth Symphony*. Take some time to listen to it if you can. It opens with a crashing dissonance, all the voices in the orchestra shouting at each other. Then begins a musical search conducted by the cello section, a search that ranges through all the themes of the previous three movements, until the celli finally settle on the tune that we all know.

Once they find that tune, the orchestra sings it four times: first the cello section with quiet reverence, then the middle strings but this time with a lovely bassoon descant, then the high strings join in, with the lower strings singing the bassoon's descant (my favorite moment), and finally, the whole orchestra rises in its triumphant rendition. You really should listen to it—it is breathtaking in its beauty (if music isn't your thing, think of an awesome sequence of plays at a Super Bowl, or the unfolding discoveries in biology over the past hundred years). One song in many voices, a song that never gets old because a musical genius has given it such rich expression.

This is what the psalms are. One great song, true, but a song taken up by many voices. Our encounters with the psalms don't always resonate because we forget this. We come to them expecting, perhaps even demanding, to find ourselves mirrored there, but this doesn't always happen (the psalms aren't always "about us"). But when we reckon with all the voices to be found there—not just the different voices in a psalm like the one we just considered but the range of voices across cultures and time, a deeper resonance settles in. We are lifted out of ourselves and into a broader, less isolated, world—the rich and diverse world of the church Jesus loves and means for us to love too. We taste a little bit of heaven.

AN EXERCISE

I have an exercise for you. Pick a psalm, or a portion of a psalm. Any psalm or portion will do, as long as it doesn't resonate with you at the moment. Now think of someone you know, or heard about on the news, for whom those words are likely to be particularly relevant because of what they are going through. Pray for that person, using the words of the psalm. And invite Jesus to join with you in that prayer.

Don't rush. Give it time. As you pray, ask Jesus to break you out of yourself. It will do you good. More importantly perhaps it will do that person good. It will make the world a better place. God will hear. Heaven will sing. Jesus will be glad.

Heavenly Redeemer, by your cross and Spirit, you have made me one with you and with every other believer across time and across the world. I don't always feel it, but it remains true. I have a shared story with you. And I have a shared story with all of my brothers and sisters, with those I know and those I have yet to meet: with Moses, with David, with my friends and even my enemies in the church. For Jesus lived, died, rose, and prays to unite us. Thank you for those moments when I have delighted in this bond, and thank you for the day ahead when I will delight in it fully.

Forgive me for those times when I think only of my own joys, plans, and sorrows. Forgive me for those times when I isolate myself from others and from you. By your Spirit, make my love stronger. Amen.

20

Reading a Psalm with Jesus

Psalm 76

In Judah God is known; his name is great in Israel.

(Ps 76:1)

Up to this point, I have been largely cherry-picking the psalms for our encounters with Jesus—either listening for his voice in the interplay of multiple voices (as we did in chapter nineteen), or meeting him in particular experiences that the psalms document—like trusting, suffering, and vindication (this we have done throughout the book).

In the present chapter, I will dispense with cherry-picking and tackle a psalm in its entirety, aiming to sharpen your skill for meeting him throughout a psalm by modelling a way to do it. I will make use of Ps 76 as I do so.

Here is how we will proceed. After having you read straight through the psalm, marking it up in a number of ways, I will model how to engage it section by section. As I do so, I will ask two questions of each section: (1) How might Jesus have processed these words as he reflected on them; and (2) How might we respond to Jesus in the light of our answer to the first question. When I get to the final section of the psalm, I will leave these tasks to you with a few suggestions.

Answering the first question will call for some speculation, which is why I will ask, "How *might* Jesus have processed these words?" But I will not be simply making things up, because we know a good bit about the story and the thinking of first-century Jews (more about that in a moment) and because we know a great deal from the Gospels of what Jesus thought about himself and his mission. As I model responding to Jesus (the answer to the second question), I won't ignore what we know from the Gospels, but I will try to stay close to the psalm, allowing the words we find there to make Jesus vivid to us.

JESUS' WORLD

Here is something of what we know about Jesus' world. That world was a restless and disappointed one—no longer exiled in a foreign land but still feeling exiled because it was subject to foreign rule despite a tantalizing moment of liberation under Judas Maccabaeus two hundred years earlier.

Jesus' world was still as apt as ever to fall into sin despite the reforming zeal of those like the Pharisees, who taught that strict adherence to God's law and purity of temple worship would summon God to rescue Israel and return her to glory and prominence. It was also a world that fostered angry zealots who were ever ready to use violence to bring back Israel's former dominance and liberty, together with upper-class assimilators, like the Sadducees, who were relatively comfortable with the status quo. Jesus' world, lastly, was insular, a world that had lost sight of its mission to love and draw in political and social outsiders.[1]

READING PS 76

Read Ps 76 through in its entirety, preferably aloud, praying for insights into Jesus' heart and mind as you imagine him processing it in the setting we have just described.

As a way of breaking the ice for the reflections that follow, *circle* phrases that you can easily hear Jesus saying, recalling as you do things Jesus did or said that make it easy for you to circle those phrases. *Underline* the statements that you find difficult to imagine Jesus saying and reflect on how he

1. See Wright and Bird, *World*, 108–41, for a fuller account of the first century Jewish world. See Stott, *Basic Christianity*, 31–61, for a succinct summary of Jesus' claims and character.

might have wrestled with them and why. Ask yourself what concerns they might have raised in his mind and what prayers and choices they might have generated.

In Judah God is known;
his name is great in Israel.
His abode has been established in Salem,
his dwelling place in Zion.
There he broke the flashing arrows,
the shield, the sword, and the weapons of war.

Glorious are you, more majestic
than the mountains of prey.
The stouthearted were stripped of their spoil;
they sank into sleep;
all the men of war
were unable to use their hands.
At your rebuke, O God of Jacob,
both rider and horse lay stunned.

But you, you are to be feared!
Who can stand before you
when once your anger is roused?
From the heavens you uttered judgment;
the earth feared and was still,
when God arose to establish judgment,
to save all the humble of the earth.

Surely the wrath of man shall praise you;
the remnant of wrath you will put on like a belt.
Make your vows to the LORD your God and perform them;
let all around him bring gifts
to him who is to be feared,
who cuts off the spirit of princes,
who is to be feared by the kings of the earth. (Ps 76:1–12)

MEETING JESUS IN PS 76

Reflect with me now on the psalm section by section, making use of our two questions. Note that whenever words from the passage appear in my reflections, I will flag them in italics.

First section (verses 1–2)

In Judah God is known;
his name is great in Israel.
His abode has been established in Salem,
his dwelling place in Zion. (Ps 76:1–2)

First question: How might Jesus have processed these words? (Note that I will answer the question by imagining Jesus praying through the passage.)

> *In Judah*, my tribe, *you are known*, Father—in David's songs, in Solomon's wisdom, and in the faithful prophets. *Your name*, Father, *is great in Israel*—in our story, and throughout our land, in the long history of your faithfulness to us. Your *dwelling place* is *in Zion*, in Jerusalem, and in the temple, where I went to learn as a boy and where we gather for worship and at our great annual festivals.[2]
>
> And now, Father, you are here in me as I make my way through *Israel*, through Galilee to the north and Judea to the south. In me you are making yourself *great* and *known*, in every word I say as I preach the gospel, as I teach, rebuke, and warn, and as I celebrate your name and welcome outsiders. You are *great* and *known* among us in all that I do—as I feed, heal, deliver, console, and bring back from the dead those we love.
>
> For these great things I praise you, Father. But will the people you and I love hear and see you in me? What will you do, what must I do, to awaken them?

Second question: How might we respond to Jesus in the light of what we have just "overheard"? (Note that I will answer this question by crafting a prayer. There are other ways you might do it.)

> Lord Jesus, your Father, the Creator of all things, has chosen to make himself *great*—clear, vivid, beautiful—in Israel's story, a story that culminates in you. To see you, Lord Jesus, is to see him. And what we see is altogether beautiful.

2. God set aside Judah to rule the nation and the world (Gen 49:8–12). He set his love on Jerusalem (Zion—see Ps 48) and filled the temple at its consecration (1 Kgs 8:1-11, esp. 10-11). God spoke through David's songs (2 Sam 23:1-3) and governed through Solomon's wisdom (1 Kgs 3:3–13), a wisdom so great that foreigners were dumbfounded by its fruits (1 Kgs 10:1–13). Jesus learned and taught at Jerusalem's festivals (see Luke 2:46–47 and John 7:37–39).

> You show us that your Father desires our company, for you came not to punish us but to *dwell* with us. You fully entered our story. You came from heaven to *Judah* and gave us a vivid account of yourself in the Gospels, so that we could see what God is like. You came kindly, with gracious words and deeds, putting up with a staggering amount of chosen ignorance and abuse from us. You came with great compassion, using your strength to heal and deliver us. You came truthfully, telling us what we need to know, even if we don't want to hear it—but always for our good. And you are a welcoming God who made yourself *great in Israel* and made your *dwelling place*—your home—*in Zion*, but only for a while. Your Spirit now dwells in the hearts of your people worldwide. Make yourself and the Father greater and greater, Lord Jesus, in and through us.[3] Amen.

Second section (verses 3–6)

> There he broke the flashing arrows,
> the shield, the sword, and the weapons of war.
> Glorious are you, more majestic
> than the mountains full of prey.
> The stouthearted were stripped of their spoil;
> they sank into sleep;
> all the men of war
> were unable to use their hands.
> At your rebuke, O God of Jacob,
> both rider and horse lay stunned. (Ps 76:3–6)

First question: How might Jesus have processed these words? (Note that, as before, I will try to answer this question by imagining Jesus praying through the passage.)

> Father, by David and many others, you *broke . . . the weapons of war*, bringing peace to this land and city. You overthrew our Greek oppressors. Long before them, you sent a plague to the armies of Sennacherib as they proudly laid siege to Jerusalem so that overnight they perished. Before that, you *stripped* the Syrian army *of their spoil*, so terrifying them in the night that they fled

3. What Jesus "began to do and teach" (Acts 1:1) during his days among us he has continued worldwide and from the inside out after Pentecost (see Acts 2, John 16:5–15, and the promise of Ezek 36:22–32).

from before the gates of Samaria, leaving everything behind. Long before those great moments, by your hand the army of Pharaoh *sank into* the *sleep* of death, *rider and horse . . . stunned* beneath the waters of the Red Sea.[4]

And now, Father, here I am, David's son, called to do battle once again with your enemies. What shall I do? How shall I break *the flashing arrows, the shield, the sword, and the weapons of war* and bring peace to *Judah* and *Zion*? Will I simply repeat what has happened before? Shall I summon the army of God if I am arrested? Shall I cheer on my disciples if they draw swords at my arrest? Will that accomplish what is finally necessary or will I need to forge a different path? Shall I be a new kind of David—the king who suffers violence in order bring it forever to an end?

Second question: How might we respond to Jesus in the light of what we have just "overheard"? (Once again, I will answer in the form of a prayer.)

Lord Jesus, thank you that did not raise an army to destroy the Roman occupiers. Thank you that you told Peter to put away his sword and prayed for your tormentors' forgiveness. Thank you that you bore violence in your own body rather than inflict it on your enemies. Thank you that you *strip the stouthearted of their spoil* not by ripping it from their hands but by changing their hearts so that, like Zacchaeus, they gladly return what they have extorted. Thank you that you subdue your enemies by turning them into your friends, that your kindness leads people to repentance, that we love because you first loved us. Thank you that you died for me when I was your enemy and I am now reconciled to you and the Father. Thank you that you will one day fill our world with peace and remove all that stands opposed to it. Help me now, in the meantime, to be more of a peace maker.[5]

Third section (verses 7–10)

But you, you are to be feared!
  Who can stand before you
  when once your anger is roused?

4. See 2 Kgs 19:32-36 for the defeat of Sennacherib's army and 2 Kgs 6:24—7:20 for the flight and despoiling of the Syrians. Exodus 14–15 documents the drowning of the Egyptians and the rejoicing that followed.

5. See Matt 26:47-56, Luke 23:34, Luke 19:1-10, 1 John 4:19, Rom 5:10, Rom 2:4, Isa 11:1–9, Rev 21:1–8, and Matt 5:9.

> From the heavens you uttered judgment;
> the earth feared and was still,
> when God arose to establish judgment,
> to save all the humble of the earth.
> Surely the wrath of man shall praise you;
> the remnant of wrath you will put on like a belt. (Ps 76:7–10)

First question: How might Jesus have processed these words in prayer?

> Father, so many in Israel fear the Romans; but they don't *fear you.* They will weep for me but won't think to weep for themselves. I have sought repeatedly to gather them under the wings of my love and protection, but they have refused. I have wept for them and warned them. And soon it will be worse for them than it was for Sodom and Gomorrah. How will they be able to *stand before you?*[6]
>
> But I fear you, Father. I love what you love and hate what you hate. I hate lying and hypocrisy, cruelty, and injustice. I love *the humble of the earth* because you do, and I surrender my glory wholeheartedly for their rescue and well-being. I love to feed the hungry and heal the sick. I love to restore the lonely and welcome all who turn to you. I love to speak the truth, whatever it costs me. I *stand before you*, prepared to do whatever it takes to throw down the *wrath of man,* and transform it to *praise.* Please use me, Father, to bring those I love back under your good reign.[7]
>
> Father, I fear for the world. Everywhere I look, inside and outside of Israel and down the ages, I see no awareness of the day when all will be *still* under your *just rule.*[8] I see only arrogance and indifference. Rome, like Egypt, Assyria, Babylon, and every oppressor before her, ignores and defies you. The Herods claim your mantel

6. Jesus laments Jerusalem's misplaced tears ("Weep for yourselves" [Luke 23:28]), coming destruction (Luke 19:41–44), and refusal to repent ("O Jerusalem . . . How often would I have gathered your children together as a hen gathers her brood under her wings, and you were not willing!" [Matt 23:37]). He warns severely: "It will be more tolerable . . . [for] Sodom than for you" (Matt 11:24).

7. Jesus obeys from the heart: "My food is to do the will of him who sent me" (John 4:34). So passionate is he regarding what God loves and hates that he unleashes invective on those who misrepresent him (see Matt 23:25–36). He heals and socially restores the woman with the flow of blood (Mark 5:21–34), befriends the lonely Samaritan woman (John 4:1–26), transforms Zacchaeus (Luke 19:1–10), and speaks the truth to his enemies (John 8:39–47).

8. When God "establishes judgment" (Ps 76:9), he does much more than execute judgment; he sets up his reign. Though v. 9 speaks in the past tense, it anticipates the future.

while murdering one another and enslaving my people for their building projects.[9]

My own people, and not just their oppressors, have chronically resisted your will and reality. There is no end to our[10] folly. We think that by violent insurrection or by strict adherence to our own version of Torah, we can force your hand. Our shepherds are hypocrites, clean on the outside but on the inside full of dead men's bones. They make up regulations that exempt them from the obligations that really matter while weighing the people down under burdens they can't bear. They forbid healing on the Sabbath. They despise the world outside of Israel, despite your merciful intention that the families of the world should be blessed in Abraham's offspring.[11]

What is to become of us? *Your anger is roused* against us. *Who can stand* before it? Spare us, O God. Use me to awaken my beloved countrymen, and people worldwide, to your reality and the folly of ignoring you. And, Father, since those I love are such slow learners, receive my faithful life in substitution for their less than faithful ones. Bring your *anger* down upon me, so that they *will be able to stand* when I come at the end of history to *save the humble of the earth.* Fill them with godly *fear* as they begin to see what I will do for them. And fill them with your Spirit after I have died and risen, so that love banishes their fears, making them winsome ambassadors. Through them teach the world to *fear* you.[12]

9. The nation fell into civil war immediately after Solomon died. God commissioned Isaiah, as he did so many prophets, to serve a people who would never listen (see Isa 6:9–13). We witness Jesus' grief in Matt 23:37 ("O Jerusalem . . . the city that kills the prophets") and his fury in John 2, where "making a whip of cords, he drove them all out of the temple" (John 2:15).

10. I imagine Jesus using "we" and "us" not because he was himself guilty of anything but because he chose fully to identify with the sins of his people, submitting to John's baptism, though he did not need to (Matt 3:13–15).

11. See Matt 23:1–36, Luke 13:10–17, and Gen 12:1–3.

12 Jesus awakens us with warnings: see Matt 11:21–24 ("Woe to you, Bethsaida . . . It will be more bearable on the day of judgment for Tyre and Sidon than for you" [Matt 11:21, 22]) and Luke 12:5 ("Fear him who, after he has killed, has authority to cast into hell"). Jesus repeatedly declares that he must suffer and die (see Matt 16:23 and elsewhere) and explains why in Mark 10:45 ("The Son of Man came . . . to give his life as a ransom for many") and at the Last Supper (see Matt 26:26–29). Paul declares our acquittal in Rom 5:1–11. Jesus promises his transforming Spirit and his enabling mission in Matt 28:18–20 and Luke 24:46–49. We see Jesus' promise come alive in Acts 2:37–47 and 1 Thess 1:4–10.

Second question: How might we respond to Jesus in the light of what we have just "overheard" in Jesus' prayer?

> Jesus, I worship you, for you, alone among us, lived out your days in godly *fear*, faithful under the hand of God. You loved him and surrendered to his will in every thought, word, and deed. You had no reason to collapse under his *anger*, and yet you did. For you took my chosen ignorance and my arrogance upon yourself as if they were your own so that I would not have to bear that load when God brings me to account. And you did it because you saw that I would never be able to *stand before* [God's] *anger*, and it broke your heart to contemplate my ruin. How deeply you have loved me and love me still. Conquer my fears with the greatness of your majesty and compassion. Turn my *wrath*—my complaining and anger—to *praise*. Teach me to love you and the Father above all things.

YOUR OWN WORK

There remains one final section in the psalm. Take some time to continue the exercise on your own. You will find some suggestions under each heading.

Fourth section (verses 11–12)

> Make your vows to the LORD your God and perform them;
> let all around him bring gifts
> to him who is to be feared,
> who cuts off the spirit of princes,
> who is to be feared by the kings of the earth. (Ps 76:11–12)

First question: How might Jesus have processed these words? The following thoughts and questions may help.

- You can either imagine Jesus speaking these words directly to you (reminding you of your "vows"—say, at your baptism) or imagine him reflecting on promises he has made to the Father (his "vows"—what might they be?), or both.
- The words seem to have the whole world ("the kings of the earth"), and not just Israel (or the church), in view.
- How might Jesus have conceived of "cutting off the spirit of princes:" As killing them? As killing the arrogance in them?

Second question: How might you respond to Jesus in the light of what you have just imagined? (I recommend answering this question in the form of a prayer.) A question to consider:

- How might you respond to Jesus, knowing that he has the whole world on his heart?

Lord Jesus, you know that what I have sought to do in this exercise is not easy. My mind is too easily distracted by my own story and problems. My historic imagination needs stretching. But you love me and are more eager to meet me in this psalm than I am to meet you.

Thank you for inspiring the psalmists—for bringing your heart and story into their words. And thank you for planting your Spirit in my own heart and imagination. Thank you that because of him the deepest part of me genuinely wants to see what the psalmists only partially saw and is able to see even more than they saw. Please continue to shine your light in me. Make your dreams and desires more and more vivid to me as I meet you in the psalms. And write those dreams and desires on my heart. I pray for your name's sake. Amen.

21

Making the Psalms a Window

And we all, with unveiled face, beholding the glory of the Lord, are being transformed into the same image from one degree of glory to another.

(2 Cor 3:18)

The psalms won't always resonate with you. But sometimes they will leap off the page. "Yes," you will find yourself crying out, "that is exactly how I am feeling right now! That's what I am going through!"

This is great when it happens. But, if you have been reading this book with any care, you know that such resonance won't always happen. And it will never be enough. What I have been repeatedly saying is that something else will need to happen if you are going to draw the deepest life out of such moments: you will need to meet Jesus in them. If you don't, the psalms will be little more than mirrors—ways of seeing yourself. And if that is all that happens, you won't change. You need to see the Savior in the psalms, not just yourself, the point that Paul makes in 2 Cor 3:18, when he speaks of us being "transformed from one degree of glory to another" *as we behold the Lord.*

The psalms *are* a mirror, to be sure. They are our songs. But they are *also* a window by which we see the Person who has come to rescue us from ourselves.

In this chapter, the third in our "practicum" on meeting Jesus in the psalms, you will roll up your sleeves more than you have yet done and set yourself the task of making the psalms into windows. You will look for Jesus in a range of them.

EXERCISE IN HISTORIC IMAGINATION

What follows is a series of excerpts from the psalms, some of them discussed in this book. They are arranged in contrasting pairs, one featuring a "downside" experience and its partner more positive. They are paired in keeping with 1 Pet 1:11, where we read that the Spirit of Christ was in the prophets predicting both the "sufferings of Christ" and his "subsequent glories."

Pick a pair, at least one partner of which resonates with your present experience. Take all fourteen if you dare—but space them out over at least a week, two or three each day. Do with them what you did in the previous chapter. That is, imagine Jesus processing them at some point during his time with us. To what events, either actual or anticipated, might the words of the psalm have been particularly relevant for him?

Circle phrases you can easily hear Jesus saying, given what you know of his life and teaching. *Underline* the phrases that you have difficulty imagining Jesus saying, and reflect on how he might have wrestled with them and why. What hopes or concerns might both sets of phrases have raised in his mind? What prayers might they have generated? What choices might they have urged upon him? Pray as you reflect, asking Jesus to engage with you.

Once you have finished imagining Jesus working with the text, take some time responding to what you have discovered about him from the exercise. You might write a prayer or a reflection.You might write a poem and set it to music if you have the gifts for that sort of thing. Or you might enhance your experience by singing the psalm in question (*The Psalter Hymnal*—see the bibliography—has them all set to music) and then just praying spontaneously off the words of the text you have chosen. You might close your session (or each of your sessions, if you decide to do all the suggested psalm portions) with the prayer at the chapter's end.

As you undertake this exercise, you might want to work with a three-column chart. The first column will contain the text you are contemplating, the middle column will contain what you imagine Jesus' reflections to have been, and the third will contain your responses to what you have discovered about Jesus. The chart might look something like this.

The Passage	Jesus' Reflections	My Response

There is no cookie-cutter approach to what you will be doing. In some cases it might be easy to hear Jesus in the words; in other cases it will not be. The goal is not to "get it right" but to engage in a practice that will do you an enormous amount of good as you get better at it.

WINDOWS ON THE MESSIAH: HIS SORROWS AND JOYS

Desolation and Rejoicing

O LORD, why do you cast my soul away?
Why do you hide your face from me?
Afflicted and close to death from my youth up,
I suffer your terrors; I am helpless.
Your wrath has swept over me;
your dreadful assaults destroy me.
They surround me like a flood all day long;
they close in on me together.
You have caused my beloved and my friend to shun me;
my companions have become darkness. (Ps 88:14–18)

I love the LORD, because he has heard
my voice and my pleas for mercy.
Because he inclined his ear to me,
therefore I will call on him as long as I live.
The snares of death encompassed me;
the pangs of Sheol laid hold on me;
I suffered distress and anguish.
Then I called on the name of the LORD:
"O LORD, I pray, deliver my soul!"
Gracious is the LORD, and righteous;
our God is merciful. (Ps 116:1–5)

Fury for God and Quiet Trust in God

Oh that you would slay the wicked, O God!

O men of blood, depart from me!
They speak against you with malicious intent;
your enemies take your name in vain.
Do not I hate those who hate you, O LORD?
And do I not loathe those who rise up against you?
I hate them with complete hatred;
I count them my enemies. (Ps 139:19–22)

O LORD, my heart is not lifted up;
my eyes are not raised too high;
I do not occupy myself with things
too great and too marvelous for me.
But I have calmed and quieted my soul,
like a weaned child with its mother;
like a weaned child is my soul within me. (Ps 131:1–2)

Grieving over the Church and Rejoicing in World Renewal

O God, you have rejected us, broken our defenses;
you have been angry; oh, restore us.
You have made the land to quake; you have torn it open;
repair its breaches, for it totters.
You have made your people see hard things;
you have given us wine to drink that made us stagger . . .
Oh, grant us help against the foe,
for vain is the salvation of man!
With God we shall do valiantly;
it is he who will tread down our foes. (Ps 60:1–3, 11–12)

Oh sing to the LORD a new song;
sing to the LORD, all the earth . . .
Declare his glory among the nations,
his marvelous works among all the peoples . . .
Worship the LORD in the splendor of holiness;
tremble before him, all the earth . . .
Let the heavens be glad, and let the earth rejoice;
let the sea roar, and all that fills it;
let the field exult, and everything in it!
Then shall all the trees of the forest sing for joy
before the LORD, for he comes,
for he comes to judge the earth.
He will judge the world in righteousness,
and the peoples in his faithfulness. (Ps 96:1, 3, 9, 11–13)

Betrayed by a Friend and Delighting in God's People

For it is not an enemy who taunts me—
then I could bear it;
it is not an adversary who deals insolently with me—
then I could hide from him.
But it is you, a man, my equal,
my companion, my familiar friend.
We used to take sweet counsel together;
within God's house we walked in the throng. (Ps 55:12–14)

Behold, how good and pleasant it is
when brothers dwell in unity!
It is like the precious oil on the head,
running down on the beard
on the beard of Aaron,
running down on the collar of his robes!
It is like the dew of Hermon,
which falls on the mountains of Zion!
For there the LORD has commanded his blessing,
life forevermore. (Ps 133:1–3)

Complaining About Enemies and Reveling in Vindication

Hear my voice, O God, in my complaint;
preserve my life from dread of the enemy.
Hide me from the secret plots of the wicked,
from the throng of evildoers,
who whet their tongues like swords,
who aim bitter words like arrows,
shooting from ambush at the blameless,
shooting at him suddenly and without fear.
They hold fast to their evil purpose;
they talk of laying snares secretly,
thinking, "who can see them?"
They search out injustice,
saying, "We have accomplished a diligent search."
For the inward mind and heart of a man are deep. (Ps 64:1–6)

They confronted me in the day of my calamity,
but the LORD was my support.
He brought me out into a broad place;
he rescued me because he delighted in me.

The LORD dealt with me according to my righteousness;
according to the cleanness of my hands he rewarded me.
For I have kept the ways of the LORD,
and have not wickedly departed from my God. (Ps 18:18–21)

Avoiding God and Coming Clean

For when I kept silent, my bones wasted away
through my groaning all day long.
For day and night your hand was heavy upon me;
my strength was dried up as by the heat of summer. (Ps 32:3–4)

Blessed is the one whose transgression is forgiven,
whose sin is covered . . .
I acknowledged my sin to you,
and I did not cover my iniquity;
I said, "I will confess my transgressions to the LORD,"
and you forgave the iniquity of my sin. (Ps 32:1, 5)

Desperate for God and Enjoying God

My God, my God, why have you forsaken me?
Why are you so far from saving me, from the words of my groaning?
O my God, I cry by day, but you do not answer,
and by night, but I find no rest. (Ps 22:1–2)

I will bless the Lord at all times;
his praise shall continually be in my mouth.
My soul makes its boast in the LORD;
let the humble hear and be glad.
Oh, magnify the LORD with me,
and let us exalt his name together. (Ps 34:1–3)

Lord Jesus Christ, I rightly worship you as my Lord. What I often find more difficult is to welcome and look to you as my fellow traveler. But you are human, fully so, and the Father urges me to love and trust you for this choice.

Your love for me as an elder brother astonishes and consoles me when I take it to heart. There is nothing abstract about it: you are fully engaged with me, fully empathetic. You know what it is to be a creature, delighting in your maker and his works, enjoying his company, and putting yourself with joy and fullness into his hands. You know how it feels to have friends and to be at peace with them. You also know how it feels to be betrayed and disappointed by people, to live with limited understanding, and to face uncertain tomorrows. You know what it is to live all your days under the cloud of mortality, in a world made ill by false gods and human cruelty. You know how hard it is to depend upon God for life and vindication in such a world. You know how hard it can be for me to set my hopes in God's promises of a brighter tomorrow. You know how to fight off the temptation to be insular, to be consumed, as I tend to be, by my own plans, needs, and fears. You know how to trust, obey, and cry desperately to God when he is nowhere to be found and every consolation is stripped away. You have felt and had your heart broken by the hatred and cruelty of enemies. Though you never sinned, you have felt what unrelieved guilt does to our bodies and spirits. You have been forsaken by God. And all that you have embraced and endured was for my sake, so that I could come to you for help.

Thank you, my brother, my friend, and my God. I bless you. I trust you. I love you. Amen.

22

The Love That Has Always Been

Then I said, "Behold, I have come; in the scroll of the book it is written of me: I delight to do your will, O my God; your law is within my heart."

(Ps 40:7–8)

I HAD A FRIEND in grad school who coordinated an arts festival. He reported that it was lots of fun. But it was also an enormous amount of work. At the end of the last plenary session, one of the participants, a musician and theologian whom he admired, abruptly bounded up to the podium and publicly thanked him. He was so immersed in the event, and so greatly enjoying it, that the thought of being thanked had not crossed his mind. But it meant a lot to him when it happened.

On Easter and at the ascension, the Father did something much grander but in one way similar. He rose to the podium, in this case a cosmic one, and, in the presence of all things and every person, seen and unseen, he honored his Son. He declared, in effect, "You have honored me, and so, by these acts of my mighty love, I honor you. You have glorified me, and so, now and forever, I glorify you." Jesus had spoken of this exchange of love and honor in his final prayer:

> Father, the hour has come; glorify your Son that the Son may glorify you . . . I glorified you on earth, having accomplished the work that you gave me to do. And now, Father, glorify me in your own presence with the glory that I had with you before the world existed. (John 17:1, 4–5)

THE EMBEDDED STORY IN THE PSALMS

I have been saying throughout this book that this is the story embedded in the psalms. It is a story about deep divine love, a love that predated the love expressed in the relationship between God and the psalmists, a love that predated God's love for you and me, and a love that came to its richest expression in the story of Jesus years after the Psalter was completed.

What I have yet to do, and what I will do in this final chapter, is to show how the gospel, as seen through the lens of the psalms, sheds light on the love that has always been—not so much the love that God has toward you and me, as the love that God enjoys within himself—particularly the love between the Father and the Son. This is a love into which God has kindly brought us. But it stands on its own and always will. It is for this reason unshakable. It doesn't need you or me to be full or complete.

There was a time in Western culture when family honor carried deep significance. When a child sullied the family name by his behavior, it grieved the family and undermined their respect in town. When a father committed a public crime, the family suffered disgrace. Remnants of this ancient value remain, often in horrific parody, as when there is a Mafia murder over a family insult.

But within the Trinity, there is no parody—only deep and eternal respect of each Person for the others. We see this in the psalms.

THE SON'S LOVE FOR HIS FATHER

Think first of the love of the Son for his Father. Picture him looking down upon the world that God had made, and especially upon us, the creatures whom God had made in his image, creatures whose essential purpose was to show forth what God is like. What does he see?

> The LORD looks down from heaven on the children of man,
> to see if there are any who understand,
> who seek after God.

> They have all turned aside; together they have become corrupt;
> there is none who does good,
> not even one. (Ps 14:2–3)[1]

The sight stirs the Son with grief, and even anger, for he sees his Father's name repeatedly ignored. Worse, he sees his Father's reputation repeatedly dragged through the mud by creatures wearing badges that say, "I am the image of God. When you look at me, you get to see what God is like." The Son knows how good, faithful, wise, patient, benevolent, and loving his Father is, and it grieves him beyond words to see him so terribly maligned by us, those who are supposed to be his representatives.

And so, the Son says, "Father, all those false sons, even the religious ones, shame you and grieve me. Let me go as one of them to rescue your honor: 'Lead me in the paths of righteousness for your name's sake' (Ps 23:3). Let me be the true Son, the image of God in human form. Let there be, at long last, a man fully worthy of the name." We hear the Son making this pledge in Ps 40, a pledge attributed to him in Heb 10:

> In sacrifice and offering you have not delighted,
> but you have given me an open ear.
> Burnt offering and sin offering
> you have not required.
> Then I said, "Behold, I have come;
> in the scroll of the book it is written of me:
> I delight to do your will, O my God;
> your law is within my heart."[2] (Ps 40:6–8)

The Son chooses to become one of us as an act of supreme and continuing devotion, a sacrifice of praise from the inside out. His food will be to do the Father's will and to show forth the Father by every word, deed, attitude, and gesture. Listen to the Spiritual, "Prepare Me One Body" (accessible on the internet), and you will feel something of the beauty and wonder of this choice: "Prepare me one body, like man. I'll go down and die."

1. Though the Gospels do not record Jesus saying these words, he certainly knew them, and he knew them to be an accurate account of our condition. Jesus "did not entrust himself to [people] . . . for he himself knew what was in man" (John 2:24–25).

2. Heb 10:5–10 puts these words in Jesus' mouth, using the Greek version of the Bible (the Septuagint), which changes "but you have given me an open ear" (Ps 40:6) to "but a body you have prepared for me" (Heb 10:5) to explain the purpose of the incarnation: "Consequently, when Christ came into the world, he said, 'Sacrifices and offerings you have not desired, but a body you have prepared for me'" (Heb 10:5).

A DEVOTED LIFE

The Father accepts the Son's pledge, and so the Son becomes a human child, Mary's baby. And thanks to the psalms, we get to see and even experience something of how fully his heart engages in this undertaking. Through them, we get to discover that the incarnation was for Jesus no abstraction, no mere doctrine but a lived out, beautiful, arduous pilgrimage of love.

Witnessing Jesus' dedication

- We witness Jesus' solidarity with us in the hardships of mortal life:

  For all our days pass away under your wrath;
  we bring our years to an end like a sigh. (Ps 90:9)

- We behold his heart-felt dedication to God and his love for righteousness:

  One thing have I asked of the LORD,
  that will I seek after:
  that I may dwell in the house of the LORD
  all the days of my life,
  to gaze upon the beauty of the LORD
  and to inquire in his temple. (Ps 27:4)

  Oh that my ways may be steadfast
  in keeping your statutes! (Ps 119:5)

- We feel his hope at the prospect of God's joyous reign over the earth:

  Let the heavens be glad, and let the earth rejoice;
  let the sea roar, and all that fills it;
  let the field exult, and everything in it . . .
  For [you come] to judge the earth. (Ps 96:11–12, 13)

- We hear his love for God-honoring worship and his declarations of purity and innocence:

  Oh, magnify the LORD with me,
  and let us exalt his name together! (Ps 34:3)

  For I have kept the ways of the LORD,
  and have not wickedly departed from my God. (Ps 18:21)

- We overhear his quiet trust in the face of bitter persecution and powerful enemies:

  When I am afraid,
  I put my trust in you.
  In God, whose word I praise,
  in God I trust; I shall not be afraid.
  What can flesh do to me? (Ps 56:3–4)

- We witness his quiet submission in death:

  Into your hands I commit my spirit. (Ps 31:5)

- We feel his delight at the prospect of joyfully sharing his victory with us:

  I will tell of your name to my brothers;
  in the midst of the congregation I will praise you. (Ps 22:22)

Witnessing Jesus' Pain

- We hear Jesus' cry of dismay as liars in growing numbers viciously accuse him:

  More in number than the hairs on my head
  are those who hate me without cause. (Ps 69:4)

- We feel Jesus' grief as he is abandoned and betrayed:

  You have caused my beloved and my friend to shun me. (Ps 88:18)

- We hear Jesus desperately appealing to God in the face of mounting horror and misery:

  Hear, O Lord, when I cry aloud:
  be gracious to me and answer me . . .
  Hide not your face from me. (Ps 27:7, 9)

- We are confronted by Jesus' bodily pain as he endures, despite his innocence, the exhaustion and debilitation that unrelieved sin brings upon the body:

  For when I kept silent, my bones wasted away
  through my groaning all day long.
  For day and night your hand was heavy upon me;
  my strength was dried up as by the heat of summer. (Ps 32:3–4)

- We recoil at the punishment Jesus willingly takes on, despite his innocence:

> Add to [me] punishment upon punishment;
> may [I] have no acquittal from you.
> Let [me] be blotted out of the book of living;
> let [me] not be enrolled among the righteous.
> (Ps 69:27–28)

Before reading on, take a moment to conduct an experiment. First, read aloud each of the bullet point headings, but skip over the quotations from the psalms. Then read the entire section aloud again, this time *with* the quotes alone (deleting the headings), thinking of Jesus as you do. I suspect that you will notice that the first read-through grows tedious—like reciting a grocery list. But I suspect that the second read-through will grab your attention, perhaps even stir your heart a bit. And I suspect that the reason for the impact will be Jesus himself, whose Spirit lives in you, who inspired the psalms (rather than the list), and who intends for you to meet him in them.

THE FATHER'S DELIGHT

Think now of the Father's love for the Son. The Father hears the Son's words of trust, joy, dedication, and grief throughout the course of Jesus' life. And he delights in the love they reveal, so much so that when, on the Mount of Transfiguration, Peter blurts out the suggestion that Elijah and Moses be honored alongside Jesus, the Father fiercely rebukes him: "This is my beloved Son; listen to *him*" (Mark 9:7).

Jesus' words and life also cause the Father to scorn any who would seek to raise a rebellion against the reign of his Son.

> The kings of the earth set themselves,
> and the rulers take counsel together,
> against the LORD and against his Anointed, saying,
> "Let us burst their bonds apart
> and cast away their cords from us."
> He who sits in the heavens laughs;
> the Lord holds them in derision.
> Then he will speak to them in his wrath,
> And terrify them in his fury, saying,
> "As for me, I have set my King
> on Zion, my holy hill."(Ps 2:2–6)

Jesus' songs so warm the Father's heart, sung as they are in the midst of the relentless testing brought about by human brokenness, cruelty, and unbelief, that when, at last, Jesus' chosen work is done, the Father vindicates him with mighty acts of cosmic deliverance:

> In my distress I called upon the LORD;
> to my God I cried for help.
> From his temple he heard my voice,
> and my cry to him reached his ears.
> Then the earth reeled and rocked;
> the foundations also of the mountains trembled
> and quaked, because he was angry . . .
> And he sent out his arrows and scattered them;
> he flashed forth lightnings and routed them.
> Then the channels of the sea were seen,
> and the foundations of the world were laid bare
> at your rebuke, O LORD,
> at the blast of the breath of your nostrils.
> He sent from on high, he took me;
> he drew me out of many waters. (Ps 18:6–7, 14–16)

So full of joy is the Father at his Son's life-long and perfect obedience that he surrounds him with the songs of his friends, the brothers and sisters redeemed by that obedience:

> I will pay my vows to the LORD
> in the presence of all his people,
> in the courts of the house of the LORD,
> in your midst, O Jerusalem.
> Praise the LORD! (Ps 116:18–19)

NOT ABOUT US

The true Son's love for the Father and the joy-filled Father's vindication of his beloved Son: This is what we get to see in the story of Jesus' life, death, and resurrection made vivid through the psalms. And of course, the Holy Spirit figures ceaselessly in this great dance as well. He enables us to see and hear Jesus in the psalms. When we call Jesus Lord, and when we call God Father, it is by the Spirit and with his delight.[3]

3. See 1 Cor 12:3; John 14:26; 16:12–15; Rom 8:15–17.

We might almost say that our redemption is a by-product of eternal Trinitarian love. We are the sideshow: God himself is the main event. But of course, that would not be quite right. For the display of Trinitarian love in the story of the gospel was no mere performance; it was an actual redemption. God truly did love us in and through this astonishing display of love within the Godhead. Jesus died not just to obey his Father but to rescue you and me. God raised his Son not just to honor his Son but to justify and raise you and me in him. And the Holy Spirit convinces us of the Father's and the Son's love because he wants you and me inside their embrace.

But there is nevertheless a sense in which our salvation is incidental to the story of Jesus and the Father. You and I need to keep remembering that life is not all about us. It never has been. This is where Adam got things wrong and where all our problems began. Life is really all about God. God loves us. But he doesn't need us. He didn't create us because he was lonely. All the love God has ever needed dwells within the community of the Father, the Son, and the Holy Spirit.

LOVE IS REAL

Thinking this way may be new to you—and humbling, perhaps. But it will also be deeply encouraging to you if you reflect on it. For it will make vivid to you that love is real, not because you make it so, or wish it to be so, but because God is love, unshakably so. All your aspirations to make love work, together with all your griefs over love not working (think of the psalms!), have meaning. They arise from the fact that love, holy love, beautiful love, astonishing love, has always been and will always remain, even if you and I are not yet very good at it.

Notice something else equally encouraging, astonishing in fact—something I have been repeatedly calling your attention to throughout the book. God may not *need* us (he doesn't, in fact), but he *wants* us. He "desires" (Ps 132:14) to make his home with us, a state of heart echoed by Jesus in John 17:

> Father, I desire that they also, whom you have given me, may be with me where I am, to see my glory that you have given me because you loved me before the foundation of the world. (John 17:24)

How astonishing that Jesus "desires" us to be with him and the Father, to be caught up in the love that has always been. But he does. He prays for it earnestly.

SOMETHING TO SING ABOUT

What follows is a hymn based on Jesus' prayer in John 17. Entitled simply "John Seventeen," we might just as well call it "The Psalms' Deep Song." You can sing it to the tune of "Jerusalem" by C. H. H. Parry, made famous in the classic film *Chariots of Fire*.

O holy Love, you've always been,
Long before our rise and sin,
Content within your joint embrace
Before the dawn of time and space.
You had no need for human praise
To fill your courts and warm your days.
For you yourself are Family,
Eternal love, the Trinity.

And yet you formed us for your heart,
Dust, yet Godlike—set apart:
Formed through your Son for your delight,
And given breath by Spirit's might.
And when your warning word we spurned
Yet still your love could not be turned.
Our crime: Your image to deface.
Your plan: To glorify your grace.

Your zeal, dear Son, drove you to say,
"Father, I, as man, obey."
With steady heart you kept his word
When every other child demurred.
Then toward the cross you set your face,
The blight of evil to erase.
Alone in darkness there you cried,
Your Father's justice did abide.

Your zeal, O Father, stretched your arm,
Drew your Son from hell and harm.
Your pow'r then raised him from the dead,
Declared with joy that he is Head.

He is the Prince of your delight,
Ascended to the highest height,
Beloved from all eternity,
The one to whom we bow the knee.

O, Spirit, raising Jesus' fame,
Joyful whene'er we own his Name.
You cry out, "Abba," as we cry,
Your joy to lift the Father high.
You write God's law upon our hearts,
You make complete what he imparts:
O, self-effacing God, content
The Son and Father to present.

We stand transfixed by what we see:
Love within the Trinity.
Your love that needs no love from us,
The self-regarding heirs of dust.
But you have kindly brought us in,
The Father's own, the Son's dear kin.
Your Spirit's witness draws us home.
The cross assures we're not alone!

Oh, help us love with your great love!
Make our joy like yours above!
May all who know us gladly view
All things made one at last in you!
Praise God, from whom all blessings flow!
Praise him, all creatures, here below!
Praise him, above, ye heavenly host!
Praise Father, Son, and Holy Ghost![4]

SPECTATORS AND PARTICIPANTS

Spectators of a great love, we become, through our union with Christ, participants in it. And this brings us full circle in our engagement with the psalms.

Let me explain what I mean by coming full circle. Think of our experience with the psalms. We begin by reading them, instinctively, as our own songs. And this makes sense because they are so personal. But then, as we

4. Composed by the author and in the Public Domain.

keep reading the psalms, we discover that they don't always easily fit what we are going through or feeling.

This disjunction, assuming we keep engaging the psalms, pushes us to listen for other voices in them to help us make sense of them. As we listen more carefully for those other voices, we encounter a deeper and broader story—the story of God's engagement with people everywhere and, most consolingly, his love for us in Jesus. We encounter, as we hear Jesus processing the psalms, a love that has chosen fully to share the experience of human life with us and has done whatever is necessary to draw us with him fully into the life of God. This love, made so vivid and beautiful as the Spirit of Christ opens the psalms to us, fires up our own faith and love. And so, at last, we receive the psalms back as our own songs, sung now in greater depth and with deeper hope.

SOME PARTING ADVICE

So what, practically, will you do with the psalms now that you have read this book? I hope very much that you will keep reading them—and that you will read them even more frequently. I hope that you will make a habit of reading all of them, not just your favorites (some people read five a day so that they can cycle through the whole Psalter every month). I hope that you will make the psalms your strong medicine for daily health—that you will wrestle with them, that you will mull them over repeatedly, and that you will engage them creatively, setting them to music, singing them, and praying them.

And as you engage them in all these ways, I hope that you will listen carefully, at multiple levels: I say "listen" to encourage you to read the psalms aloud as much as you can. Making them audible will help you hear them better.

Listen first for the voices of the original writers: enter their world, for they are your fellow pilgrims and have a story to tell in their own setting that is worth listening to. Enjoy your solidarity with those who lived and called on God long before your time. It will take you out of yourself, and that's a good thing.

Listen as well for your own voice, for these songs are yours too, songs that the Spirit has given you to supply you with rich (even at times surprising) expression for your own joys, sorrows, and aspirations. If you are not presently going through what the words describe, think of those you know or imagine who are. Pray with and for them, for these songs are *ours*, not just *yours*, and are meant to bind us together worldwide.

But never neglect to listen for the voice of Jesus. Let the actual words of the psalms (not just the ideas those words articulate) show you Jesus' heart as he chose to live out a truly human life alongside you. Thank him for the sorrows, aspirations, and delights that are so richly articulated in the psalms—sorrows, aspirations, and delights that he freely chose so that in the end he could offer his life in substitution for yours. Thank him as well that the richness of those freely chosen experiences means that you can talk to him about anything and everything. And then *do* talk to him about anything and everything.

It will not always be easy to meet Jesus in the psalms, but the more you give yourself to that task, the clearer he will become. And the more vividly you encounter him, the more your hope will rise and the more fully you will resemble him.

Glorious Trinity, you are love and have always been. You do not need me, for fullness of relationship exists within you. But you choose to love me, even to desire me. I wonder at your determination to draw me into your embrace. I wonder at your choice, eternal Son, to empty yourself and to dwell among us here in our broken, angry, and ungrateful world as our servant. I wonder at the cost of the cross, where, heavenly Father and Son, your matchless love for one another endured a sundering that I cannot measure as you atoned for my sins. I wonder, blessed Holy Spirit, at your incalculable kindness to me: you delight to show me your love; you delight to use the psalms to convince me of the love of the Father and the Son for me. You have been patiently and irresistibly writing your love and goodness on my heart, teaching me to love the Son as the Father does and to love the Father as the Son does, teaching me to love my friends and family and enemies the way you love me.

Almighty God, how comforting it is to me to know that love is real. How comforting it is to know that that love is mine, that that love belongs to those fellow believers whom I love, and that I have a God who longs for my company and who has done all that is necessary to secure it.

With all my brothers and sisters across time and space, I praise you, LORD! I praise you in your sanctuary; I praise you in your mighty heavens! I praise you for your mighty deeds! I praise you according to your excellent greatness! I praise you with trumpet sound; I praise you with lute and harp! I praise you with tambourine and dance; I praise you with strings and pipe! I praise you with sounding cymbals; I praise you with loud clashing cymbals!

Let everything that has breath praise the LORD! Praise the LORD!

Bibliography

Boersma, Hans. *The Hermeneutics of Tradition*. Eugene, OR: Cascade, 2014.

Brown, Peter. *Augustine of Hippo: A Biography*. Berkeley: University of California Press, 1967.

Cameron, William. *Informal Sociology: A Casual Introduction to Sociological Thinking*. New York: Random House, 1963.

Dawkins, Richard. *River Out of Eden: A Darwinian View of Life*. New York: Basic, 1995.

Frost, Robert. "The Death of a Hired Man." In *North of Boston*, 14–23. New York: Henry Holt, 1914.

Goldsworthy, Graeme. *Preaching the Whole Bible as Christian Scripture*. Grand Rapids: Eerdmans, 2000.

Hillenbrand, Laura. *Unbroken*. New York: Random House, 2010.

Kelly, Thomas. "Stricken, Smitten, and Afflicted." In *The Trinity Hymnal*, 257. Atlanta: Great Commission, 2000.

Kidner, Derek. *Psalms 1–72: An Introduction and Commentary on Books I and II of the Psalms*. Downers Grove, IL: InterVarsity, 1976.

———. *Psalms 73–150: A Commentary on Books III-V of the Psalms*. Downers Grove, IL: InterVarsity, 1975.

Lane, William. *The Gospel of Mark, The New International Commentary on the New Testament*. Grand Rapids: Eerdmans, 1974.

Lewis, C. S. *The Great Divorce*. New York: Macmillan, 1966.

———. *Perelandra*. New York: Macmillan, 1967.

Longman, Tremper, III. *How to Read the Psalms*. Downers Grove, IL: InterVarsity, 1988.

Murphy, Kate. "No Time to Think." *New York Times*, Section SR (July 27, 2014) 3.

Newton, John. "Amazing Grace." In *The Trinity Hymnal*, 460. Atlanta: Great Commission, 2000.

———. "Glorious Things of Thee Are Spoken." In *The Trinity Hymnal*, 345. Atlanta: Great Commission, 2000.

Noel, Caroline. "At the Name of Jesus." In *The Trinity Hymnal*, 163–64. Atlanta: Great Commission, 2000.

The Psalter Hymnal. Grand Rapids: CRC, 1988.

Shakespeare, William. "King Lear." In *William Shakespeare: The Complete Works*, edited by Alfred Harbage. Baltimore: Penguin, 1969.

———. "Macbeth." In *William Shakespeare: The Complete Works*, edited by Alfred Harbage. Baltimore: Penguin, 1969.

Stott, John. *Basic Christianity*. Downers Grove, IL: InterVarsity, 2008.

Tolkien, J. R. R. *The Return of the King, Part III: The Lord of the Rings*. Boston: Houghton Mifflin, 1965.

The Trinity Hymnal: Revised Edition. Atlanta: Great Commission, 2000.

WCF. *Westminster Confession of Faith: A New Edition,* edited by Douglas F. Kelly, Hugh McClure, and Philip B. Rollinson. Greenwood, SC: Attic, 1981.

Willcocks, David, and John Rutter, eds. "Tomorrow Shall Be My Dancing Day." In *100 Carols for Choirs*. Oxford: Oxford University Press, 1987.

Wilson, Timothy D. "Just Think: The Challenges of the Disengaged Mind." In *Science* 6192 (2014) 75–77.

Wright, N. T. *The Case for the Psalms: Why They Are Essential*. New York: HarperCollins, 2013.

Wright, N. T., and Michael F. Bird. *The New Testament in Its World*. Grand Rapids: Zondervan Academic, 2019.

Yancey, Phillip. *Church: Why Bother*? Grand Rapids: Zondervan, 1998.

www.ingramcontent.com/pod-product-compliance
Lightning Source LLC
LaVergne TN
LVHW050643100826
845148LV00011B/1958

9798385266463